STARTING SPIRITUAL DIRECTION

A GUIDE TO GETTING READY, FEELING SAFE, AND GETTING THE MOST OUT OF YOUR SESSIONS

JOHN R. MABRY

Apocryphile Press

1700 Shattuck Ave #81, Berkeley, CA 94709

www.apocryphilepress.com

Copyright © 2017 by John R. Mabry

Printed in the United States of America

ISBN 978-1-944769-95-6

All rights reserved. No part of this book may be reproduced, stored in a retrieval
system, or transmitted in any form or by any means—electronic, mechanical,
photocopy, recording, or otherwise—without written permission of the author
and publisher, except for brief quotations in printed reviews. Printed in the United
States of America

Quotation from St. Ignatius from *Ignatius of Loyola: Spiritual Exercises and Selected
Works*, edited by George E. Ganss, S.J. (Mahwah: Paulist Press, 1991).

Quotation from Meister Eckhart from *Meditations with Meister Eckhart* (Santa Fe:
Bear & Co, 1983) by Matthew Fox, p. 15.

Please join John R. Mabry's readers' group at
BookHip.com/FNQCMX
and we'll send you a FREE BOOK!

CONTENTS

INTRODUCTION

When Sally came into my office, she looked a little lost. "Where should I sit?" she asked.

"Anywhere you like..." I said, but then I lowered my voice, "...although I *usually* sit there." I pointed to a chair.

She smiled and took the other, but she didn't look any more at ease.

I lit a candle and said, "This will remind us that there are three of us here." The large window of my office looked out onto the busy Berkeley street, but inside there was a feeling of spaciousness and calm. "Let's just take a few minutes to truly arrive and find our center," I invited her. I closed my eyes and relaxed, offering a quick prayer asking the Divine to fill the space between us, and to help me pay attention—both to Sally and to the Divine. After a couple of minutes of delicious silence, I said, "Amen." I opened my eyes and saw Sally sitting just as rigidly as before, looking twice as anxious.

"Welcome to spiritual direction," I said.

"Thanks," she said, "What do we do here?"

That is a million-dollar question—one that everyone has the first time they enter a spiritual direction session, whether spoken or unspoken. Sally's question snagged me, though, and wouldn't let me go. "Sally should have something to read to prepare her for this work," I thought. I looked around for something of the sort, but while there are lots of books out there for spiritual directors, there didn't seem to be any user-friendly guides for spiritual direction *clients*.

That's hardly a challenge any writer can ignore, and so this book is for Sally and for everyone else new to spiritual direction who would like to be better informed about the ministry, what it can do for them, what they can expect, how they can feel safe, and how they can get the most out of their sessions. If that's the position you're in, then this book is for you.

Spiritual direction is an amazing ministry, completely unlike any other. It is personal, intimate, and non-coercive. In your spiritual director, you will find a soul friend, a fellow companion who will walk beside you on your spiritual journey, and help you unpack your spiritual experiences, discern important choices, parse long-held beliefs, and nudge you gently toward growth.

Spiritual direction isn't always comfortable—anytime we get close to a truth we'd rather not see, a part of us wants to run screaming. That's okay. Spiritual direction provides safe space to uncover such truths. It also gives us the only place in modern society where we can talk about our mystical experiences without people thinking we're crazy! In fact, it is in spiritual direction that we learn that such experiences are normal, and we can begin to explore what they mean, and the kind of life they are inviting us to.

And that's just the tip of the iceberg. When I say, "Welcome to spiritual direction," I'm saying a lot. I'm saying welcome to the place where your soul is well and truly cherished and safe.

A COUPLE OF THINGS ABOUT THIS BOOK

I intended this book to be short, but I also tried to include everything in it that you need to know before stepping into a spiritual direction session for the first time. By the time you finish it, you will have a good grasp on what this ministry is about, what you can expect in a session, what you can expect from your spiritual director, and how to make sure you make the best use of your time. It was a balancing act to include all that was needed while still keeping it short and user-friendly! I may not have done it perfectly, so if you have questions I didn't answer (or didn't even think of) please don't hesitate to email me. I will send you an answer and may address your question in a subsequent edition of the book.

One thing that people who are very familiar with spiritual direction may find strange is that I don't use the word "directee" to refer to those receiving spiritual direction (folks like you, presumably). That was a very conscious choice. "Directee" is an "insider" word—outside of the world of professional spiritual directors the word is not used and has no meaning. One might argue about whether it is a legitimate word at all. Certainly, people who have never been to a spiritual direction session will not be familiar with this word. Instead, I use the word "client," with which everyone is familiar and most people are comfortable. The only people not comfortable with it are old-time spiritual directors, but that's okay because this book is not for them! No doubt some of them will argue that I could just explain what the word means. I have done so, but...I am still not going to use it. The truth is I can't stand the word "directee"—I find it clunky and obscure and elite.

One of my early readers objected to the use of the word "training," preferring "formation." While I agree that formation is a much better word for what we do in a spiritual direction certificate program, it is also an "insider" word that may not be familiar to those who are being introduced to this ministry for the first time. Again, I choose to opt for the word that will be immediately understandable to the widest number of readers.

Another choice I made was to refer to spiritual directors throughout using the feminine gender. I was about a quarter of the way through this manuscript when I wrote the mind-bogglingly awkward sentence, "He or she is a professional, and if his or her space is not professional, his or her business will suffer." That's when I started thinking, "This may not be the way to go about this." To avoid such unnecessary clunkiness in the prose, I decided to speak of all spiritual directors using the pronouns "she" and "her" rather than "he or she" or "his or her." The fact is that there are far more women than men doing spiritual direction —and most of us men who do it are pretty in touch with our inner feminine—so I don't expect many protests. I apologize to any of my fellow male spiritual directors who might take offense, and invite them to write their own books full of awkward and clunky prose.

Finally, some thank-yous are in order. Great thanks to the Rev. Anne Jensen, Rev. James Ford, and Ravi Verma for reading the first draft of this book and offering much helpful feedback.

Now that such housekeeping is out of the way, let's talk about spiritual direction...

LET'S TALK ABOUT SPIRITUAL DIRECTION

WHAT IS SPIRITUAL DIRECTION?

There isn't one answer to this question. And any answer I could give would be incomplete. A poetic answer might be: two souls basking in the Divine Presence. A clinical answer might be: a helping profession in which the director assists the client in his or her spiritual flourishing. A theological answer might be: one beggar showing another beggar where to find bread (Martin Luther's definition of ministry in general).

But for the purposes of this book I'm going to say: In spiritual direction, two or more seekers enter sacred space to dream, explore, and discern a path toward personal wholeness and deeper intimacy with the Divine. Usually this journey is a one-to-one, face-to-face meeting, with one seeker acting in service to the other. Often, they speak. Often, they don't.

Along the way, they talk about just about everything that happens in life—work, play, relationships, personal struggles—but always the question comes back to a central question: how is the Divine wooing us, calling us into deeper and deeper intimacy?

As we go deeper, more questions emerge: What is the Divine "up to" in all of our daily ups and downs? How is the Divine moving and nudging and forming us, through both our triumphs and our defeats? How do we resist the Divine call? How does the Divine's desire for intimacy threaten us and push us beyond our comfort zones? What does this intimacy require of us? What is it calling us to? In what ways are we out of congruence with the deepest truth of our souls—with this Divine calling—and how does this imprison us and limit us? How can we move into deep places of interior freedom that are transformative and healing and liberating, not only for us, but for the world?

Those are Big Questions. Spiritual direction is often the only place in our lives that many of us have to deeply explore such questions, witnessed by another soul, without judgment or condescension. It is the place where we can be encouraged and challenged to open ourselves more deeply than we ever thought was possible. This is deeply healing work.

One metaphor that I like is that of the spiritual director as couple's counselor. The couple, of course, is you and the Divine. Both of you want deeper intimacy, but how do you get there? Intimacy is scary, and often the things that get in our way aren't even conscious. The spiritual director is there to hold the space, to speak what she notices, and to help guide you and the Divine into the kind of deep and meaningful connection that you both desire.

Spiritual direction is also a place to work through big decisions in our lives, where we can consider which choices are most in congruence with our soul, with our deepest longings, and with the sacred covenants we have made.

A word that is very important in the spiritual direction community is "discernment." Whether we are discerning the Divine will for our lives, how the Divine is showing up in our lives, how the Divine is challenging or wooing us, or whether we are discerning life changes large or small, discernment is a primary focus in any spiritual direction session.

WHAT IF A PERSON DOESN'T BELIEVE IN GOD?

People of many faiths—and none—are discovering that spiritual direction is a helpful ministry for them. Theistic traditions (those who believe in a personal, conscious deity) often use the language of love and romance to discuss the kind of relationship the Divine wants to have with each of us. The mystics of the world's religions often practice what is called "love mysticism." They write about how the Divine is wooing the soul of the poet, who in turn longs for his or her Beloved. It is because of this common trope in theistic traditions that we employ the language of "intimacy" when describing the goal of spiritual direction.

Yet what is intimacy about? It's about connection and union. While non-theistic traditions—such as Buddhism and humanistic nature mysticism—don't speak of "intimacy" they do speak of connection with all beings and the unity of all being. Yet this, too, is a kind of intimacy.

"Connection" and "unity" are useful concepts and they often arise in spiritual direction. But for the purposes of this book we are going to emphasize the concept of "intimacy" because there is a quality inherent in that word—a sweetness and a longing—that is simply not present in the other terms.

It is difficult to find words that apply across the spectrum to people of every conceivable belief system, so I ask non-theists to make this small translation: when I say "intimacy" please hear "connection" or "union"—but coming from a deep place that every human heart cries out for.

WHAT LEADS A PERSON TO SPIRITUAL DIRECTION?

Many things can lead a person to seek spiritual direction. Sometimes people have powerful mystical experiences that they don't understand or can't explain, and they need a safe space to explore their import. Sometimes people are wrestling with difficult beliefs, or have been spiritually wounded and want to heal. Some people are in the process of changing beliefs and need support as they sort through what they will keep and what they will discard. Other people have important life choices to make and want to make sure they are listening to their deepest wisdom before they make a commitment.

All of these are common, but most commonly people come to spiritual direction simply because they want to grow closer to the Divine, they want a richer, more fulfilling spiritual life, or they want support as they deepen their spiritual practice.

This will change, too. Often a person will come for one reason, but a year or two later, a different reason will emerge. Spiritual direction is a flexible ministry that can meet us where we are at, and can continue to support us as we grow and change spiritually.

HOW IS SPIRITUAL DIRECTION DIFFERENT FROM THERAPY OR PASTORAL COUNSELING?

On the surface, spiritual direction and psychotherapy often look very similar. Two people meet in an office. They talk for an hour. Then they make an appointment for their next meeting. Usually payment is made. The client leaves and another client comes.

But that's where the similarity ends. In psychotherapy, the therapist and client are focused on the client's emotional life. But in spiritual direction, the spiritual director and client are focused on the client's spiritual life. Also, people usually enter therapy because they are experiencing some difficulty in their lives, usually as a result of emotional wounding or trauma. But in spiritual direction, we do not assume there is a problem.

Sure, sometimes people go to spiritual direction because they have a specific spiritual problem or issue they want to work on, but mostly we just assume that people come to spiritual direction because they want to go deeper in their spiritual practice and move into a place of deeper intimacy with the Divine.

Many people confuse spiritual direction and pastoral counseling, but there are important differences. Just as with therapists, people go to pastoral counselors because they are experiencing some kind of problem in their lives, and they are looking for help and support from a pastoral advisor whom they trust to use the resources of their faith—scripture, tradition, and theology—to help them reach a resolution.

Because pastoral counseling is crisis-oriented, it is short-term. A person might meet with her pastoral counselor two or three times, until a way through the crisis has been found. Spiritual direction, however, is not crisis-driven, and it is usually long-term. A client might see her spiritual director for many years, often more than ten years!

Certainly, there will be many crises discussed in spiritual direction during those ten years, but the crisis will never be the center of the discussion—that will always be the lure of the Divine into greater and greater intimacy. The spiritual director may discuss how the crisis is affecting that intimacy, or how the Divine is moving within or through the crisis in order to call the client into greater intimacy, but intimacy will always be the center point of the discussion.

Nevertheless, spiritual direction is a highly specialized form of spiritual guidance, and spiritual guidance comes in many forms. Many of us, at some time in our lives, have received important spiritual guidance from parents, teachers, therapists, counselors, 12-step sponsors, and even random strangers. Spiritual guidance can come from pretty much anyone! The ministry of spiritual direction is both similar to and different from all of these: while spiritual guidance can come in many forms, spiritual direction is a very focused, intentional, and (usually) long-term helping relationship.

A SHORT HISTORY OF SPIRITUAL DIRECTION

Spiritual guidance is as old as human spirituality itself. As soon as human beings began to discern a spiritual dimension to life, we began to ask older and wiser members of our community for advice. Such personal mentoring is probably the oldest form of spiritual direction.

But as religions developed and became more complex, a clergy class emerged in most of them, whether this was the shaman, the rabbi, the priest or the roshi. These clergy people became the go-to folks for spiritual guidance, and in most traditions, this is still the case. They were (and are) often seen as the "experts" in the spiritual life.

Since they were seen (and often saw themselves) as experts, the traditional approach to spiritual guidance in most traditions has been pretty hierarchical. It was often patriarchal as well—spiritual guidance was usually of the "father knows best" variety. The "expert" told you what to do if you wanted to grow spiritually, and most people—those who were sincerely seeking to grow spiritually—obeyed. (While there have always been laypeople who offered spiritual guidance in most traditions, they were often marginalized and unacknowledged.)

While this "directive" approach was undeniably fruitful for many, it led to widespread abuses in most traditions—and this is equally true of both Eastern and Western religions. Spiritual leaders often imposed their beliefs on their followers, policed their doctrine, and assumed that their own path was normative for everyone. This has led to the wounding of many tender souls throughout history. In the West, the arrogance and elitism of a hierarchical approach to religion, religious instruction, and spiritual guidance has led many to leave traditional faiths in the dust (and in disgust).

But something significant happened in the 1960s and 1970s. Some Roman Catholic nuns began to forge a new way to offer spiritual guidance, which they called the "non-directive method." Informed by St. Ignatius, who counseled spiritual directors "not to lean or incline in either direction but rather, while standing by like the pointer of a scale in equilibrium, to allow the Creator to deal immediately with the creature and the creature with its Creator…" (*Spiritual Exercises*, 15).

Similarly influenced by psychologist Carl Rogers (one of the founders of humanistic or "client-centered" therapy), the non-directive method assumes the client is the expert on his or her own spiritual life, not the clergyperson or the director. The director is seen as simply a fellow traveler on the spiritual journey. The director may point out what she sees and may offer suggestions for practice, but the client is always empowered to take or leave the director's advice.

This nonhierarchical approach minimized the potential for abuse, and it was widely popular in Roman Catholic circles. The word got around, and in the late 1970s Protestants asked the nuns to train them in the non-directive method, and in the 1980s and 1990s Buddhists and Jews asked to be trained in the new method as well. Each of these later formed schools of spiritual direction themselves, teaching the non-directive method in their own religious contexts for use with their own members.

DIRECTIVE AND NON-DIRECTIVE METHODS TODAY

Today, the non-directive method is the normative technique taught in almost all spiritual direction training programs, regardless of the spiritual tradition the program is rooted in. There are nearly 250 training programs in the United States alone, of widely different traditions, which speaks to how powerful and effective the non-directive method can be.

That said, the directive method is enjoying a bit of a comeback. In our effort to get as far away from the abuses of the directive method as possible, many spiritual directors believe we have swung too far in the other direction, effectively offering little direction at all. They believe a middle ground or a "synthesis" should be sought.

In actual practice, this is exactly what happens. Some people do not need much direction—they are very much self-directed, and for them, the role of the spiritual director is largely to hold space and listen. But some clients require a little more support and a little more active guidance. This can include redirecting the client back to the subject of intimacy, offering suggestions for spiritual practice, and even assigning homework.

Most spiritual directors intuitively gauge how directive or non-directive they should be. While some spiritual directors will naturally be more directive than others, for most of us, how directive or non-directive we actually are will vary from client to client, based on the client's personality and needs.

How directive or non-directive your spiritual director will be with you will probably be intuitive, too. Of course, you may ask directly for your spiritual director to move in one direction or another. If you feel like your director is offering too many suggestions, you can simply ask them to back off. They will! Most often, though (and counter-intuitively) people find they want more structure than they are receiving. Suggestions and homework are often helpful and welcome. You can ask your spiritual director for more of those, too.

The most important thing to remember is that in the non-directive method, you (the client) are in control. Your spiritual director has no power over you. Nor does she have any authority over you. She does not know what is "right" for you, nor does she have any right to correct your thinking or your beliefs. *You are the expert on your own spiritual life*, not your spiritual director. You get to negotiate how directive or non-directive your director should be in order to receive the maximum benefits of your time together.

TRAINING FOR SPIRITUAL DIRECTORS

Training for spiritual directors is incredibly important. The non-directive method is not intuitive, and without training people quite naturally fall into advice-giving, "fixing," correcting people's beliefs, and—even more dangerous—they can fall into abusive behaviors.

The problem is that spiritual direction is not a licensed ministry. Technically, anyone can hang out a shingle and call themselves a spiritual director without any training at all. While this practice is legal, it is certainly not ethical. All responsible spiritual directors are in agreement that a person cannot practice ethically without proper training.

Training for spiritual direction is open to anyone with a genuine call to this ministry. One doesn't need a Bachelor's or Master's degree. One doesn't need to be a clergyperson. One must simply feel an authentic call and be willing to be trained. However, some training programs will not admit students who are under thirty-five years of age, because they don't feel they have sufficient life experience to direct others well. Other programs welcome even people in their early twenties. All programs will go through a discernment process to assess whether a student seems like a good candidate for the ministry.

Training programs are often of wildly different durations—some are month-long intensives, some last a year, some two years, and some even three years. Most have approximately the same number of classroom hours, however, and the difference is usually how much time there is between each class. For instance, a three-year program might meet for three hours every other week, while a one-year program might consist of four five-day intensives. The program I direct at the Chaplaincy Institute includes 120 classroom hours, 30 hours of spiritual direction, 12 hours of supervision, and 18 hours of client practice—a total of 180 hours.

You can be confident that if your spiritual director has

completed a reputable training program, she will companion you ethically and responsibly. Whether she will companion you *effectively* is another matter. That will have more to do with your personal compatibility—see more about that below.

HOW TO FIND A SPIRITUAL DIRECTOR

This is the first question people often ask me when they hear about the ministry of spiritual direction—"How do I find a spiritual director?" And just as often, "How do I find a *good* one?"

There are several ways:

- If you belong to a spiritual tradition that is familiar with the ministry, you can ask your clergy or trusted elders in your community for a referral.
- You can also call a training program in your area and ask for a referral.
- Go to the Spiritual Directors International website (www.sdiworld.org) and click on "Find a Spiritual Director." There you'll be invited to enter your postal code, and you'll soon be face-to-face with a map showing every spiritual director in your area, along with their phone numbers and religious affiliations.

I suggest you make a list of about six people from this map. Call each of them and have a short, ten-minute conversation. Choose three of these that you feel a connection with and make appointments to see them. At the end of those three appointments, you'll have a good idea which spiritual director is going to be the best fit for you.

Don't worry, you won't hurt anyone's feelings by deciding to work with one spiritual director over another. As I've stated before, spiritual directors are big on the word "discernment," and they will encourage you to discern well in finding just the right spiritual director to work with.

Please note that your spiritual director does not need to be from the same spiritual or religious background you are. Some of the best matches are of people from different traditions. For instance, I am a Christian, but I went to a Jewish spiritual director for fourteen years, and it was one of the most significant and important relationships of my life. A director outside of your own tradition can often possess a helpful distance and detachment from it that can be very illuminating. She may feel more "safe" than someone who is part of your own tradition.

(By the way, don't be afraid of nuns! Even if you're a Protestant or a Buddhist, in my experience Roman Catholic nuns are kind of wild women and amazing spiritual directors. Don't let the habit scare you off.)

During your initial interview, it's good to ask what your prospective spiritual director will charge for your time together. Please keep in mind that you are not paying for their companionship, but for their time—which is a very valuable commodity for any of us. Spiritual directors vary widely in what they charge for their time. Interns usually charge nothing, while beginning spiritual directors often charge between $25 and $50 per session. More experienced spiritual directors often charge between $50 and $100. Very experienced directors may charge even more. Directors in the heartland of the US are usually on the lower end of this scale, while directors on the coasts (where the cost of living is much higher) tend toward the higher end. Some spiritual directors consider their ministry a gift to the world and do not charge at all. These are treasured souls, but rare! Most spiritual directors must charge, as they have mortgages and bills to pay. Please remember that the "workers are worthy of their wage," and that your director's time is valuable.

Please keep in mind that the professional organization for spiritual directors, Spiritual Directors International, does not screen members. In other words, people who wake up one day and decide to call themselves spiritual directors without a single day of training can join the professional organization and can be listed on their website. The vast majority of folks listed on the SDI website have proper training, but some do not, so buyer beware. If you look for your spiritual director through the SDI website, please make sure you ask whether your prospective director completed a training program, and if so, which one.

PREPARING FOR A SESSION

*P*eople who come to spiritual direction are of all types. With some clients, I don't have to say a word. From the moment we begin they are off and running, and all I really need to do is smile and nod occasionally. (Oh, and sometimes suggest that we might be off-topic.) These are what I call "fire hose" clients—folks who are so eager for the safe space of spiritual direction that they can hardly contain themselves.

But other clients have a hard time getting started. Often, they are not used to spiritual direction and might feel intimidated by it. After all, if you've spent your whole life *not* talking about the most important relationship in your life—because you're afraid people will think you're crazy or because it isn't considered polite—just having someone say, "Okay, talk about it now," doesn't mean you can. It might take a while. And that's okay, because the space of an hour is a luxurious block of time. (Although once you get going, that hour will pass very quickly indeed.)

If you find that words don't come easily, you may have to work a little harder. Some preparation will really help with this. One thing you can do to help with this is to pay attention to the thoughts, feelings, and sensations that arise during your spiritual practice.

By "spiritual practice" I mean anything that makes you feel most fully alive or anything you do to get closer to the Divine. Perhaps this is a regular prayer time or a sitting meditation practice. It can also include forms of active meditation such as Tai Chi or walking meditation. It can even include such practices as feeding the hungry or visiting the old or infirm.

Everyone is different, and the ways we connect to the Divine will be different, too. But whatever it is you do, pay attention as you do it. What thoughts arise as you are doing your practice? In many practices, such as meditation, thoughts are sometimes seen as a distraction and something to be avoided. Yet in other forms of practice (even other forms of meditation) the thoughts that arise contain valuable information, and attention to them is part of the practice. So long as you do not let your thoughts hijack your practice session and take you out of the present moment, they can be useful no matter what your practice is.

The kinds of thoughts that arise might not make a lot of sense to you, but they can be the key to unlocking profound truths about you and your relationship with the Divine. "Why do I think about my mother's disapproval whenever I try to meditate?" or "Why do I think about sex every time I sit down to pray?" are both great questions to take to your spiritual director—and both are teeming with possibilities.

Your emotions are also a valuable guide in your spiritual journey. Does your spiritual practice leave you feeling energized or drained? Those are important feelings to take to your spiritual director. What if your spiritual practice leaves you confused or conflicted? Take those feelings to your director, too. We are whole beings, and everything in our lives can have bearing on our relationship with the Divine.

Most people get why thoughts and feelings might be important, but bodily sensations? The fact is that our bodies contain much wisdom that our conscious minds are often oblivious to. If you were to show up and say, "Every time I try to pray, I feel this pain in my left shoulder," your spiritual director would most likely be very curious indeed, and would have many questions for you—one of which might unlock a door that you never knew was there. But your body knows. And it is actually speaking to us all the time. Most of the time, however, we're not really listening. Spiritual direction can provide the spaciousness for us to let the body speak. We'll talk more about this later.

MAKE A LIST

Another thing you can do to avoid that deer-in-the-headlights "what now" feeling is to keep a running list of things you want to discuss. If you're someone who keeps a notebook or a day planner nearby, this is easy. I keep a list on my reminders app on my iPhone.

The things on this list can be anything you want to bring up with your director. If you hold a fairly conventional Jewish or Christian view of the Divine, your list might include things like these:

- What is prayer for if God already knows what I need?
- Meditation is boring. Why is it so many other people seem to get something out of it?
- I'm afraid if I tell God the truth, he'll hate me
- Whenever I try to pray, all I can think about is cheese. What's up with that?
- I don't even know what I'm feeling most of the time—how can I share that with God?
- Remind director I'll be away in July
- I think I'm allergic to spiritual community
- What if this whole God thing is delusional?

- When I think about what God wants from me, I seize up. What am I afraid of?

...And so on. If you keep a running list all month, you will have more than you can possibly discuss by the time you sit down with your spiritual director. Any theological wrestlings are fair game, as are your experiences in prayer or meditation (or other spiritual practices). Your experiences in spiritual community will also provide plenty to explore. Above all, make sure to take note of your feelings for your Divine Beloved, and whatever struggles you discover in your relationship with the Beloved.

WRITE DOWN YOUR DREAMS

Another thing you might try in preparation for your session is writing down your dreams. Dreams are often a rich source of spiritual wisdom, and most spiritual directors are eager to hear about them. The problem with dreams is that they are often ephemeral—they dissipate quickly upon waking. Writing them down the moment you wake up is a great way to preserve them. Keeping a pad and pencil near your bed will help with this.

It will also help you to dream. All of us dream whenever we are sleeping, but many people do not remember their dreams, or don't realize they have dreamt at all. Strangely, going to bed with an intention to remember your dreams can actually help you remember them!

You don't need to remember the whole dream for it to be valuable. Sometimes just an image or a feeling is enough to gain insight. Write down whatever you remember and bring it to your session.

There are many ways to approach a dream, and your spiritual director will probably have many ideas on this herself. One way of looking at it that I find valuable is understanding the dream as a symbolic snapshot of everything that is happening in your life right now. Making connections between elements in the dream and aspects of your own life can often be very enlightening.

Usually, the Divine is part of the dream. Unfortunately, the Divine is not always the "good guy" in the dream. I remember a client who said that night after night he dreamt that he was being chased through the streets by an attacker. When we finally got done unpacking the dream, the only question left on the table was, "Why are you running away from God?" It was the beginning of a much deeper vein of exploration.

Even dreams about violence or rape can have a sacred dimension. After all, rape is not just an act of violence, but is also an act of unwanted intimacy. If we have been spiritually wounded, the depth of intimacy that the Divine wants to share with us can be unwelcome and scary. The dream is often showing us in symbolic terms exactly what is going on in our spiritual lives. Spiritual direction provides a safe space to unpack dreams and interpret them, allowing us to stay focused on the questions that are uncomfortable or that we usually choose to avoid.

WHAT HAPPENS IN A SESSION?

THE SETTING

*I*deally, your spiritual director has an office—often one shared by people of other helping professionals, such as Licensed Clinical Social Workers and therapists. The setting is professional, clean, and inviting. There might be religious symbols on the wall. If your spiritual director is strongly identified with a particular faith tradition and works primarily with folks from that tradition, images from that tradition will most likely adorn the walls. If your spiritual director works with people of many different faith traditions, you might see a variety of symbols, or none.

Most likely, there will be two comfortable chairs facing each other, often with a candle set on a small table between them or to one side. There may be bookshelves, which you might be tempted to explore when your director's back is turned. If your director (or the professionals who share the office) uses tools such as sand trays or art, you will probably see those supplies.

But "ideal" is not always the norm. Not all spiritual directors have a professional office. Some of them will see you in the office they have for their "day job." If your spiritual director is also a pastor or a therapist, you will probably see them in the office they use for that job.

Just as often, however, spiritual directors see people in their homes—meaning the spiritual director's home. Sometimes she may have a "mother-in-law" cottage in back devoted to her practice, but most often you'll simply meet in her living room—one of you sitting on the easy chair, another on the couch.

Some people might be uncomfortable at first, meeting people in their homes, but in fact, this is very common. No matter where you meet your director, the environment should feel hospitable. It should be clean, uncluttered, and feel like a place you would want to spend some time in.

Spiritual direction is often spoken of as "a ministry of hospitality," and your director will take this seriously. She may offer you tea. She may offer you a sweater or a throw if it's chilly.

If you step into your director's place and it does not feel hospitable, clean, or safe, do not feel obligated to stay. Your director is a professional, and if her space is not professional, her business will suffer—and should. Simply turn to go, but later make sure you contact her to convey why you needed to leave. Your director might not understand in the moment, but once you explain, she will have the opportunity and the invitation to make her space more inviting for future clients.

More and more, spiritual directors are seeing clients in "virtual" spaces—working by Skype or Zoom or via other online platforms. While nothing beats a face-to-face meeting, these options provide a workable middle ground between working on the telephone and being there in person. But even when working online, "atmosphere" and setting are important. Your director should be well lit. The camera should be at eye-level (not staring up her nose), with an uncluttered background. Again, we're talking about ideals, and your mileage may vary. But to those of us who practice this ministry, setting is important, because we are representing the hospitality and generous welcome of the Divine itself.

BECOMING COMFORTABLE WITH SILENCE

When people first come to spiritual direction, they are sometimes baffled when the spiritual director doesn't say anything. Remember that the spiritual director's job is to hold space for you to encounter the Divine, not to actually "do" anything. Therefore, if you don't say anything, she might not either. That will leave you sitting together in silence. And for most folks in our culture, that can feel…uncomfortable.

Americans typically find silence awkward, and so we rush to fill it in any way we possibly can. If there's nothing substantive to talk about, we resort to small talk. Anything to avoid the dreaded silence.

But silence is healing. It's counter-cultural. Silence is something that most of us, deep in our bones, are deeply thirsty for. For most hours of our lives, we're being bombarded by information—the TV, the radio, the internet, billboards, children. Don't you just want to shout, "Shut up!" to the world?

Spiritual direction is safe space for silence. Many people are drawn to Zen Buddhism because they find sitting in a room full of people without talking is deeply healing in a way they don't fully understand and can't explain. Many traditions offer silent retreats for the very same reason. Spiritual direction offers another opportunity to be "alone together," in silence before the Divine.

It is likely that you and your director will talk about something during the course of your visits, but your director also knows how holy and healing silence is, and will be comfortable with it, even if you are not. And be prepared for her to say, "Let's just sit in silence with that for a moment," every now and then. Remember, you're there because you've decided to trust this person with an hour of your time—so trust her, even with uncomfortable silences. You might find that you actually enjoy them. You might even find that, deep down, you're deeply thirsty for them. Silence can be delicious.

But silence is also productive. In the *Tao Te Ching*, Lao Tzu says, "Being is what we have, but non-being is what we use. Many spokes join to create a wheel, but it is the empty space in the middle that makes it useful." Silence is an important tool in our work together because we sometimes must create space in order for something good to emerge or to reveal itself. If we're constantly barraged with noise, both inside and out, how can we hear the quiet whisperings of the Spirit? In spiritual direction, we honor silence, and we intentionally create spaces of quiet for the voice of the Divine to be heard.

THE FLOW OF A SPIRITUAL DIRECTION SESSION

Every spiritual direction session is different, and every director is different as well. Indeed, you will be different from any of your director's other clients. Yet in the midst of all this uniqueness, most sessions fall into a similar pattern.

Most sessions are between 50 to 60 minutes in length. If you have a spiritual director who does sessions that are less than 50 minutes, this is hardly worth your time, as you will not have time to truly drop into any deep discussion. On the other hand, if your spiritual director wants to meet with you for more than an hour (I have heard of sessions that have gone from an hour and a half to nearly three hours!) run the other way as fast as you can and find another director! There is nothing that is appropriate to discuss in spiritual direction that cannot be handled within the normal one-hour time range. If you need more time than that, then what you need isn't spiritual direction, but probably some other helping profession, like therapy. (I don't say that to be funny or insulting—it's simply the truth. We all need therapy now and then.)

Back to 50 to 60 minutes: Some directors (usually those who don't have a lot of clients) will do a full hour, but those who see several clients a day will probably do a "50-minute hour." This is how I work myself, so that I can schedule my clients on the hour rather than at weird times, like 10:12.

But let's say for the sake of example that your director does a 60-minute session. You and your director will greet each other and take your seats. Then your director will probably light a candle, saying, "Let this light remind us that the Divine is present with us," or something to that effect. Then she will invite you to sink into holy silence for a few minutes.

When your director says, "Amen" or some other sacred word to bring completion to your time of silence, you will probably both smile. Then your director will wait. This is your time, after all, and she will wait for a cue from you as to how you want to fill it. What are the questions that have been nipping at you this month? What are the dreams that have confounded you? This is the time to pull out your list and begin to really work on what has been emerging from your spiritual practice.

But that's not what usually happens. First, most people will go through a catalog of things that have been going on in their lives. Your director will smile and nod and may make a note or two as you list the things that have happened to you between the last time you were in that seat and today.

You might be saying, "Why would I waste the first half of my session talking about nothing?" That's a good question. I think it's like how some people can just sit down at a desk and get to work, while other people must clean the desk before they can concentrate. Some people can indeed just walk in, center, and instantly start in on the deep stuff. But most folks have to "clean the desk" first, running through the significant events of the month, as if sifting and sorting and putting things in drawers until they come across that one scrap of paper they've been meaning to show you.

This is all perfectly normal, and after a few minutes (maybe even ten or twenty) you will have caught up, the energy in the room will shift and deepen, and the real work can begin.

But what if you continued like that for the whole session? It does happen, and when it does, a red flag pops up in your director's brain and she will eventually stop you and redirect you to the reason you are there. "What does this have to do with the Divine?" she might say, and that will be your cue to refocus and get down to business.

YOUR FIRST SESSION

Many people are nervous when they enter their first spiritual direction session. This is both understandable and unnecessary. I think part of the reason they are nervous is due to a leftover fear of authority (remember waiting to go into the principal's office?) and perhaps a fear of not measuring up when speaking to clergy (your spiritual director may or may not be a clergy person, but our imaginations often put them in the "religious authority" category anyway).

There are plenty of legitimate reasons to be nervous about spiritual direction, but fear of your spiritual director isn't one of them. One of the wonderful things about this ministry is that your spiritual director is your peer, not your boss or your better or any kind of authority. She holds no power over you. This is so important in spiritual direction that it is considered unethical for your pastor or rabbi or teacher or anyone else who holds any kind of authority over you to serve as your spiritual director.

Your spiritual director is your equal, not your superior. Not in any way. She is not the expert on your spiritual life—you are. She is simply a fellow traveler who walks with you to explore the terrain. True, your spiritual director knows a thing or two about the spiritual life—she is not uninformed. She has had a lot of training in this. But she is still not considered "an authority." You hold all the authority.

At the same time, your director will be very familiar with spiritual direction, while it might be new to you—so there is much to learn. After inviting you to find your center, your director may begin by asking you what you think you're here for—in other words, what is your understanding of what spiritual direction is about?

If you have read this book, you will have an advantage when this question is asked. But your director isn't springing a pop quiz on you. Many people are very unclear on the purpose of spiritual direction when they start. Perhaps a friend suggested it but didn't explain it very well. Many people don't clearly understand why it is different from psychotherapy or pastoral counseling. Many don't know what to expect or hope for.

Your director just wants to put all the cards out on the table, so that your expectations will be realistic. You can talk about your understanding of the ministry, then your spiritual director can talk about her understanding of the ministry. In the space where your two understandings overlap, there will be plenty of space to sit and talk.

After you have agreed about what you're there for, your spiritual director may discuss your covenant with her and hers with you. (More on the contours of this covenant later in the book.) After this, your director will probably ask you the most important question of all: "What is your story?"

Your story is the history of your spiritual seeking, from your earliest memories up to the present. This history is incredibly important for your spiritual director to know. It is the context of your current journey. What has happened to you in the past will by necessity be driving what you do in the present and the future. Telling your story may be equally instructive for you. We don't always have an opportunity to tell our life story—and we almost never get to tell that story with attention to our deeper, spiritual lives.

This can be scary, but it is also liberating. I encourage you to be courageous and tell your director the things that you are most nervous about—your story is safe with her, and just in the telling you will make connections and have revelations that will surprise you. It is precisely in attempting to articulate those things that are deepest that we come to understand them—or even to be aware of them. This is part of the magic of spiritual direction.

When telling your spiritual story, be careful that you don't just give your director a list of your religious affiliations—that's playing it safe. It's a way of evading the real work before you. Sure, your affiliations are part of the story, but what your director really wants to hear about is the relationship between you and the Divine. Remember when you went on a date back in high school? The next day your friends didn't want to hear about where you went, they wanted to hear about *what happened between you*. Your spiritual director is the same way. The affiliations are nice, but what she really wants to hear is the juicy stuff. And since the juicy stuff is really what it's all about, it's best to just go there. I know, I know, intimacy is hard to talk about, especially with a stranger. But that is, in fact, what you are there for. It would be silly to go to a restaurant, order a meal, and then not eat it. Just so, it would be silly to go to spiritual direction and not talk about what is most important.

You might be saying, "I have a long story—how could I possibly tell it in one session?" Why would you need to? You might need two or even three sessions to tell your story. That is fine. Spiritual direction is not like pastoral counseling—it isn't short term. It's long term. It's a relationship that, ideally, will go on for years. The hour-long sessions are meant to be luxurious— there is no rush. You have time. Give your story as long as it needs.

Your spiritual director will probably ask you questions along the way—she isn't trying to interrupt or throw you off course. She is just trying to understand your story fully, and so will some-times need help understanding the context of an event or what it meant to you. Think of her as your partner in exploration, because in explaining things to her, you might find your own understanding deepening, and new horizons of inquiry revealing themselves.

THE KINDS OF THINGS YOU WILL TALK ABOUT

Once you've talked about what spiritual direction is for and you've told the story of your spiritual life, then what? Then the real work can begin. Only you will know what that is. And you probably won't be conscious of it. You will need to wander around a bit. Eventually, you'll intuitively hit on it.

On the other hand, you might enter the room and know *exactly* what it is you need to talk about. One thing about spiritual direction: you almost never know ahead of time what will happen in a session. It is always a surprise. Nevertheless, there are a few things that people often talk about in session. Let's look at a few of those.

Mystical Experiences. Sometimes people have spiritual experiences and they don't understand what has happened to them or why. The fact is that most people have mystical experiences now and then, but almost no one ever talks about them for fear of being labelled "crazy." This is tragic, because when these experiences happen (and they will happen to most of us) we have no context for them, we don't understand them, and we think there's something wrong with us. Nothing could be further from the truth. Mystical experiences are normal, and they happen for a very important reason.

We talk a lot in our culture about "emotional intelligence," but what we need is some training in "mystical intelligence." If we talked about mystical experiences when they happen to us, if we opened up to our friends and families and co-workers about them, then when they happen to others, they wouldn't feel scared or isolated or like some kind of freak.

But that isn't likely to happen in our culture anytime soon, so until we have a shift in culture, we have spiritual direction. Spiritual direction is the one place you can be certain no one is going to shame you or shut you down or freak out if you talk about your mystical experience, no matter how bizarre it was. This is because your spiritual director knows something that the wider culture does not: mystical experiences are not the exception, they are the norm. Your spiritual director is a safe person to talk about these experiences with—more than this, she can explain why they happen, and can help you understand why they have happened to *you*.

The fact is, most mystical experiences happen in order to get our attention. Let's let Bob illustrate this for us. Bob is a high-powered finance guy. He's all about the buck, and everything else in his life takes a back seat to his work. One day, he has a powerful mystical experience in which he feels a profound connection with all living beings—that he somehow is them, and that they are somehow him. The feeling lasts for about an hour, and after it passes, he says, "What was that?" Bob has a choice: he can shake it off as a flu symptom, or he can go deeper with it, start to explore the experience, investigate whether it was showing him something real. If he chooses the latter, it can set him off on a path of spiritual exploration that can completely transform his life, reorienting him toward the Real, connecting him to spiritual community and spiritual practice. If he ignores this Divine "invitation," however, the next mystical experience will probably be more dramatic. The Divine will keep ramping it up until it gets Bob's attention. If Bob is lucky, he will start working with a spiritual director who can both "normalize" the experience for him and also help him make the connections that will unpack the experience for him, encouraging him toward a deeper and more meaningful spiritual life.

Congruence. Bob's next task might be looking at all the things in his life, things like his work, his relationships, and his hobbies, asking himself, "Are these congruent with the spiritual insight I have received?" He might discern that some relationships are healthy and support his deeper inquiry, but others are not. He might choose to let go of some friendships and to cultivate others. He might discern that some hobbies are good for his soul, while others are not. He might begin to take a hard look at how he makes his living and ask himself whether it is "right livelihood," as the Buddhists call it. Is how he makes his living congruent with the spiritual wisdom he has received? Does his job require him to exploit others or to put them in danger? Is the corporate culture toxic to his own soul or the souls of those who work for him? Does his work endanger the planet or exploit the poor? These are deep and important questions. True spirituality isn't just about what we believe, it is also about how we live. Your spiritual director can help you discern whether the way you live is congruent with your deepest spiritual values.

Images of the Divine. Many of us were given horrific images of the Divine when we were growing up. These images might have come to us from our religious communities or sometimes just from the culture at large. We might have been told that the Divine is an exacting taskmaster, just waiting for us to get out of line so that "he" could punish us. We might have been given images that make God out to be harsh, judgmental, or intolerant. Our images of the Divine might be distorted, toxic, abusive, and perhaps even monstrous.

The problem is that once we have those images in our heads, it isn't easy to shake them. Even after we grow up we realize that the "real" Divine agent in the world can't logically be anything like the image we were given as a child, there's no "undoing" the old image, just like we can't "un-see" a car accident. We'll always be traumatized by it to some degree.

But if we come to spiritual direction to become more intimate with the Divine, we must somehow deal with these images. No one can cozy up to a monster or a demon or an abuser—why would we want to? And if those are the only images for the Divine that we possess, we might run screaming from spiritual direction, even though our souls long for a deeper connection.

Spiritual direction can help. Your spiritual director can ask where these images came from, how we feel about them, how they trigger us. She can help us identify and objectify the image and find other, more accurate, images—healing images.

I remember one client I once had who had been given the most horrible image of the Divine by his fundamentalist childhood church. Once we discerned that this image was still kicking around and causing trouble, I asked him, "Why do you need this old God? Why don't you fire his ass and hire a new one?"

His eyes widened. "You mean I can do that?"

"Let's fill out a pink slip for him," I said. "Let's do it right now…"

We never completely get rid of these old images, but our spiritual directors can help us find a better, more useful place for them. For myself, my childhood god is on my trusted inner council of advisors. He's no longer in charge, but he often has good advice (he's an amazing judge of character—who knew?). He's not going away, but now he has a new job. He's working for me, rather than against me. I now have a better, much more loving relationship with the Divine. And the image of the Divine that I now hold bears little resemblance to my childhood god.

That's healing work.

Spiritual Practice. Spiritual direction is amazingly helpful when it comes to spiritual practice. It is safe space to talk about what's working—or not working—in your spiritual practice. Let's say, for instance, that you are having trouble meditating. What's going on? Meditation used to come easily to you, but now it seems like a chore? That's a good thing to bring to your spiritual director. Together you and she can explore what has changed, shifted, or challenged you spiritually that might be affecting your meditation practice. Your difficulty might be a normal stage on the way to a deeper breakthrough, or there might be an area of incongruence that is tripping you up. Your spiritual director can help you explore what's happening.

Perhaps your prayer life is taking off, and you are having feelings you have never experienced before. Spiritual direction is safe space to explore those feelings, to give thanks for your deepening prayer, and to inquire what these new feelings are inviting you to.

Your spiritual director can also hold you accountable for your spiritual practice. You might have the best of intentions to do your Tai Chi routine every day, but something always seems to come up. But if you know your spiritual director is going to ask, "So how's the Tai Chi going?" it might just get you off your butt and making those cloud hands. That can be helpful.

Theological Questions. Another common topic in spiritual direction are theological wrestlings. Your spiritual director is probably not a religious scholar, but even if she is, rending fatwas or religious judgments on things is not her job. Nor is policing your beliefs. (More on this later.) She is not there to tell you what is right or wrong about your beliefs. Your beliefs are *your* beliefs, and her opinion doesn't enter into it. Your spiritual director can, however, provide a sympathetic sounding board as you explore, examine, and question your own beliefs. She can help you find logical inconsistencies, or help you reframe an old teaching in a new and life-giving way. She can encourage you to explore a belief you find scary.

Questioning old or engrained beliefs can often be scary. Your spiritual director can hold your hand during these explorations, encouraging you to go deeper when it gets frightening, and affirming that the Divine will not be angry if you actually say what you are thinking out loud. Everyone wrestles with theological questions. Even such basic questions as "Why do bad things happen to good people" is a good topic for exploration in spiritual direction. Your director will not have the answers to any of these questions. (If she says she does, you should probably find another spiritual director.) She will not impose her beliefs on you, but she can help you explore what *you* believe, and can support you as you question those beliefs.

TOOLS YOUR SPIRITUAL DIRECTOR MIGHT USE

Your spiritual director has been trained in the use of many different tools and techniques, and you will certainly experience them now and then. Many are very helpful in making discernments and tracking progress. Tools can come from many different traditions, and preferences for them vary widely among spiritual directors. Here are a few of the most common.

Art. Often our subconscious is wiser than our conscious mind. It is often aware of things that are going on within us and around us, things rattling around in our past, as well as fears for our future that we are not consciously aware of. Art is a great way to access the wisdom of our unconscious minds, to bring it to the surface, to consciousness. Your spiritual director may ask you to do some artwork, or you may take the initiative and bring some art to explore during your session. "Art" is a big category, of course, and I can't think of any categories of art that would not be appropriate to explore in spiritual direction: painting, drawing, sculpture, poetry, songwriting, fiction, dance, improvisational movement—all of these are valuable tools for spiritual revelation and discernment.

Focusing. Focusing uses the body as a tool for discernment. Most of us have had the experience of the body acting independently of the mind in order to safeguard our health. I went through a period last year where I was working so hard that I hadn't had a day off in nearly four weeks. I was running here and there maniacally, trying to fulfill all of my obligations (and to do them all perfectly, of course). Finally, my body simply had enough of it and came down with a massive cold that had me in bed for a week. It was exactly what I needed, and I have not forgotten the lesson.

My body knew what it needed, and when I wouldn't give it what it required, it simply took it—which proves that it is wiser than my mind. This is often the case, and we can use it to good effect in session. Spiritual directors sometimes use this "wisdom of the body" to get a quick "read" on a situation.

Focusing was developed in the 1960s by psychologist Eugene Gendlin as a way to bypass the conscious mind. In this method, a spiritual guide may ask a client where a thought or a feeling or a situation resides in her body. Based on the information that emerges, the body can often tell us something that the conscious mind either does not know or is actively (if subconsciously) resisting.

This method was developed further in the 1970s by Peter A. Campbell and Edwin M. McMahon, who termed their method Bio-Spiritual Focusing. Simplifying Gendlin's model, their method is very popular in spiritual direction circles.

First, the director will usually suggest Focusing in response to a matter for discernment that has arisen. The director will usually ask the client to become aware of his or her body. Then the director may say, "Where do you feel this issue in your body?" Something in the body will usually make itself known—a pain in the liver, a restless leg, a tight stomach. Whatever it is, it will most likely be obvious to you which part of your body is speaking—and maybe quite loudly!

Next, your director might ask you if there is an image or a word or a feeling that comes up for you that is related in some way to the sensation in your body. This is deeply intuitive work, so it's best to just say the first thing that comes to mind. Your director will repeat the sensation in your body and the image/word/feeling that has arisen, to make sure you feel a resonance between them.

The director will then invite you to ask the sensation, "What do you need from me? What do I need to know? What is needed for this to be okay?" Speak the information that comes forth. Then savor the feelings and the wisdom that emerges. Give thanks, if that feels appropriate.

The magic in this method occurs in the triangulation between 1) the issue to be discerned, 2) the body sensation, and 3) the image that emerges. I know, I know, talking about this process in the abstract sounds a little woo-woo, but it really can yield some amazing results. The fact is that our bodies are always talking to us—not unlike the Divine. The problem is that we rarely get quiet enough to hear them, nor do we really pay that much attention.

If this seems kind of complicated, don't worry—you don't need to remember anything. Your spiritual director will guide you through the whole process, or through just a part of it, as might feel appropriate in the moment.

For more on this method, see *Focusing* by Eugene Gendlin (Bantam, 1982), *Bio-Spirituality: Focusing as a Way to Grow* by Peter A. Campbell and Edwin M. McMahon (Loyola: 1992), or *The Power of Focusing: A Practical Guide to Emotional Self-Healing* by Ann Weiser Cornell (New Harbinger, 1997).

Dreamwork. I've already mentioned working with dreams in spiritual direction, but one of the best methods I know for doing this effectively—and one that is widely used in the spiritual direction community—is Jeremy Taylor's Projective Dreamwork. According to Rev. Taylor, "All dreams come in the service of health and wholeness." Just as in the non-directive method of spiritual direction, where the client is the expert on her spiritual life, in Projective Dreamwork, only the dreamer can say what her dream means. But if that meaning is not immediately obvious, your spiritual director might offer what she sees in the dream, using a very important formula: she must always preface her interpretation by saying, "If this were *my* dream, it would mean..."

This does something very important—it allows the spiritual director to offer possible meanings for the dream, while granting the dreamer full control over whether to accept that meaning. The director owns her own interpretation, but does not impose it on the dreamer. The dreamer might have an "aha!" moment in response to an interpreter...or she may not. Either way is okay. This creates safe space for both the director and the client to unpack and explore dreams.

Taylor says that no dream has only one meaning. Dreams are multivalent—they reveal more and more as you work with them, and can often hold many meanings, even conflicting meanings. This is perfectly normal. It is just part of the richness of this symbolic method of communication between the unconscious and the conscious mind.

For more on this method, see Jeremy Taylor's *Dreamwork: Techniques for Discovering the Creative Power in Dreams* (Paulist Press, 1993), *Where People Fly and Water Runs Uphill: Using Dreams to Tap the Wisdom of the Unconscious* (Grand Central Publishing, 1993), and *The Wisdom of Your Dreams: Using Dreams to Tap into Your Unconscious and Transform Your Life* (Tarcher, 2009).

Ignatian Discernment. Ignatius of Loyola was a Spanish courtesan in the 16th century. After catching a cannon ball in the hip, he had a long period of convalescence in which he got quiet enough to notice some very important things: his feelings. He discovered that when he read the racy novels of his day he felt depressed, but when he read the lives of the saints he felt elated. He started to pay attention to those feelings and brought them into his prayers. Later, as he developed a method of prayer he called *The Spiritual Exercises*, Ignatius encouraged people to use their feelings as a tool for discernment.

If you are trying to decide between two life choices, Ignatius says, and one choice is healthy and the other choice is unhealthy, that's an easy decision. But what if both choices are good choices? Choosing between two goods is sometimes very difficult.

Ignatius speaks of the imagination as if it were an organ of perception. So one way to use Ignatius' method is to go into prayer and fantasize before God, vividly imagining one possible way you could go. As you fantasize, pay attention to the feelings that come up. Does this fantasy create a feeling of depression or heaviness? Or does it create a feeling of buoyancy and happiness?

Next, fantasize about the other option, once again paying attention to your feelings. The option that results in the more buoyant feelings is probably the best option.

Ignatius called this method, "the discernment of spirits," calling the heavy feelings a "spirit of desolation" and the happy feelings a "spirit of consolation." (Spiritual directors will still use these terms sometimes, so now you have the decoder ring.)

Another method of discernment that Ignatius pioneered is known as the Perspectival Method. For this kind of discernment, we are once again faced with a choice between two goods (or between the lesser of two evils). First, Ignatius says, we should pray and put everything in God's hands (Ignatius was a Catholic Christian). Second, imagine what advice you might give to someone who came to you with a discernment like this. If that doesn't yield a good enough result, imagine that you are on your deathbed, many years in the future. You are looking back at this decision. What do you notice about it from the perspective of the end of life that you are not seeing now? Finally, Ignatius invites us to imagine that we are standing before God's throne on judgment day. God asks us about this decision. Does that change our perspective any?

Ignatius' methods never tell us what to do, but they do give us some very useful tools for exploring important discernments in our lives, especially when the options before us seem equally good or equally bad.

Setting intentions. Being conscious about your spiritual goals can help you achieve them. Just speaking them aloud to another person is a big step toward bringing them about. Your spiritual director can help you clarify your intentions and hold you accountable for them once you have committed to them. Your spiritual director can also give you a reality check when your intentions are not realistic.

This happens more than you think. Many times, I've seen a client decide to get "serious" about her spiritual life and inform me that she is now going to start meditating an hour a day (or some other Herculean spiritual discipline).

Because I strive to be a good spiritual director, I usually raise my hand up at this point and say, "Why are you setting yourself up for failure? Why not commit to something more manageable—like fifteen minutes? Then, if you find it's working, and you want to try for longer—like twenty minutes—you can."

Clients usually nod, realizing the wisdom of this. Your spiritual director has been around the block a few times and can often give you good advice about your intentions.

Evaluations. Every now and then, your director might say to you, "How do you think we're doing?" She might even schedule such a conversation once a year with you. This is a great opportunity to step back from your normal conversations and talk at a meta-level *about* those conversations. Have they been fruitful, helpful, challenging?

Your director will probably ask you to think back to a year ago, and then invite you to discern what kind of progress you think you have made over the last year. Has your spiritual practice deepened? Has your intimacy with the Divine deepened?

She may then ask you to imagine yourself a year from now. Where do you want to be then? What kind of progress would you like to make in the next year? This is a good time to set your intentions regarding your working relationship for the next twelve sessions (assuming you meet monthly), adjust your expectations, and communicate openly and honestly with your spiritual director about what you expect from her in the next year.

And so much more… The few tools listed above just scratch the surface of what you might find useful in your sessions. Your spiritual director will probably have some favorite tools of her own to suggest as well. A comprehensive exploration of such tools would require a book of its own. But I do encourage you to be open to new ways of looking at and exploring your spirituality, and to be open to methods your spiritual director might suggest. Even if they might seem a little odd or uncomfortable at first, you might be surprised at how fruitful they are.

SUGGESTIONS & HOMEWORK

Your spiritual director's primary job is holding space and listening. But every now and then she may make a suggestion. You might even ask her for one. This is just fine. But one thing to keep in mind is that your director's suggestion is just that—a suggestion. It isn't an order. You are still the expert on your spiritual life and you are still in control.

Before making a suggestion, your director will usually ask permission. She might say something like, "Can I make a suggestion?" If you say "yes" (and you probably will), take her suggestion seriously, but don't feel bound to it in any way. You don't need to commit to it, either. All you need to say is, "Thank you for that." You can follow up on it...or not, depending on whether you thought it sounded helpful.

Something that will require a commitment—or a refusal—is homework. Some clients seem absolutely allergic to this word, and some really crave it and ask for it. Everyone is going to differ on this. Again, please keep in mind that this is not mandatory. Your spiritual director might say something like, "How would you feel about some homework around this?" The homework might be a spiritual practice of some kind, or an experiment. If you find the homework suggestion welcome, feel free to accept it. If not, just say, "Not right now," or something of the sort. Your spiritual director knows better than to push.

Homework differs from a suggestion in that you and your director are making an agreement—a covenant, really—that you will do the homework. If you don't intend to do it, or you don't want to do it, don't commit to it. It's as easy as that. It's a lot better to just say, "Um…I don't think so" than to have an assignment that feels onerous hanging over your head all month. It's enough to make you not want to return to spiritual direction. And in my experience, that has sometimes happened!

Just remember: this is your time. Your spiritual director will make suggestions and offer homework because she thinks it will be helpful and fruitful for you. But as always, you make the decision, and you get to say "yes" or "no."

WHAT WON'T HAPPEN IN A SESSION

*N*ow that we've got a handle on the kinds of things that happen in a spiritual direction session, let's mention a few things that definitely should *not* happen. This is not to say that none of these things have happened in a spiritual direction session—they certainly have. But they should not happen, and if you find yourself in a session where any of the following do happen, you should stop your spiritual director and tell her that you think what she just said is inappropriate. If she apologizes and agrees, and if you feel safe enough, stay. Your spiritual director is human and can give in to normal human impulses now and then. But if your spiritual director pushes back or you no longer feel safe, the best thing to do is simply to get up and leave. You can explain later, if you want to, but you don't owe your spiritual director an explanation in the moment. The most important thing is for you to get clear of the room, regain your footing, and find a place that feels safe. Your spiritual director might be confused, might ask you what you're doing, and might even object, but don't let that stop you. Spiritual direction must be a place of safety, and if it stops being that, then your first priority is getting to a place of safety before trying to sort out your thoughts and feelings.

PSYCHOTHERAPY

First, spiritual direction is *not* psychotherapy. Psychotherapy is focused on pathology—what is wrong or broken or wounded within you that causes suffering in your daily life. Spiritual direction does not begin with the assumption that there is anything wrong with you, only that you want to deepen and grow. Of course, you may come to spiritual direction because you are experiencing a problem, and you and your spiritual direction may need to discern whether the proper place to deal with that particular issue is in spiritual direction or therapy.

Second, psychotherapy is focused on your emotional life. Spiritual direction is focused on your spiritual life. We are whole people, and often there are not strong compartments between these areas (especially if we're reasonably healthy). It is a matter of focus. In therapy you will be focused on relationships with human beings, healthy interactions, and discovering and eradicating patterns of thinking and reacting that no longer serve you. In spiritual direction you will be focused on your relationship with the Divine, establishing healthy interactions with the Divine (spiritual practice), discovering beliefs and ideas that no longer serve you, and replacing them with those that do. So...similar...but different. Spiritual direction is solidly focused on the Divine.

Depending on your situation, you may need to work with both a spiritual director and a psychotherapist. Personally, I recommend this for everyone—I am a big believer and a staunch advocate of psychotherapy for everyone, and I see both a therapist and a spiritual director. We are all people of depth, and we can all find healthier ways of interacting and being in most areas of our lives.

Your spiritual director may discern that what you really need is therapy, not spiritual direction. If your spiritual director says something like this to you, please don't take offense. Take her seriously and go find a therapist. This is often the case if you have difficulty staying "on track" in your sessions. If you find you keep drifting into talking about your human relationships and situations, you probably need therapy rather than spiritual direction. If your spiritual director is good, she'll tell you this outright.

She is not trained in therapy, and if you bring "therapy issues" to your spiritual direction session, you are putting her in an awkward and difficult position. Some people treat spiritual direction as "cheap therapy," but that's unfair to the ministry and to spiritual directors. We have a very particular job to do—one that your standard therapist or even pastor or rabbi cannot do. (Believe it or not, offering spiritual guidance is not part of standard seminary education. Go figure.)

You may not be clear on the line between therapy and spiritual direction. That's okay. Your spiritual director will be, and she'll "train you" by gently redirecting the conversation when it drifts into therapy territory. Soon you'll get the hang of it. The shorthand, once again, is that spiritual direction is focused on your relationship with the Divine—that is the single point around which all of your conversations will revolve.

Your director may insist that in order to continue with you, she will require that you be in therapy as well. This is also common and normal. Your director isn't trying to force anything on you. Whether she wants to work with you is just as much a valid discernment as whether you want to work with her. You both may set boundaries and negotiate the rules of your covenant. If your director discerns that your need for therapy is greater than your need for spiritual direction, it is perfectly within her right to set a boundary and require you to be in therapy if you want to continue seeing her. You are perfectly free to say no and find yourself another spiritual director, but I advise you to take her suggestion (or requirement) seriously. She will not make it lightly, and she might really be on to something.

41

Get your ego out of the way and carefully discern your next steps.

If you agree and you return for another session of spiritual direction, don't be surprised if your director becomes more directive in order to keep you on target in your conversations. This is part of her job, after all.

ADVICE

Your spiritual director will never give you advice on how to live your life, how to manage your relationships, or how to invest your retirement savings. That's just not her job. She may be tempted to give you advice on your spiritual life, but if she is experienced and skilled, she won't do that, either. When I say "advice," I mean you are not going to hear your director say, "Here's what I think you should do…" That's because a) it's none of your director's business, and b) you are the expert, not her.

But what if you ask her directly? What if you are discerning a very hard life choice, and even though you've gone through several discernment tools, you find that you are still really struggling, and so you say, "What do *you* think I should do?" If your director is wise and has good boundaries, she will refuse to answer. If she is like most of us, however, she might take pity on you and relent a bit. But she will still be wise enough to say, "If this were *my* situation, here's what I would do…" That way she owns her comments for herself, but she's still not telling you what you should do.

"But wait a minute," you might say, "you just talked about suggestions in the last chapter." Suggestions and advice are different things. Advice is about the kinds of decisions you should make in life. Suggestions are about a spiritual practice you might or might not choose to try. That's a big difference and it's important to see it. With a suggestion, your director will ask permission before making it. But it makes no sense to ask permission to give advice—it will feel icky no matter how she couches it.

If you find that your director is giving you advice, you have a choice: you can confront her and see if she stops (in which case you may or may not want to continue working with her) or you can find another spiritual director. I'd give you my advice on that, but...

FIXING

Similar to advice-giving is fixing, which is just a little more pro-active. Fixing is so natural for us that we often aren't aware that we are even doing it. In fact, you've probably done it sometime in the last twenty-four hours. Whenever we are talking to someone we care about, and they mention a problem, it is second-nature for us to go into brainstorming mode to help solve the problem. We have a strong urge within us to "fix" the problem so that our friend or loved one will return to a happy and carefree state.

A quick example will show exactly the kind of thing I mean. I was commiserating with a colleague around a student who was acting out in one of my classes.

"Have you had a talk with her about it?" he asked.

"Yes."

"Did you lay out an 'if the shoe was on the other foot' scenario?"

"A what?"

"Sometimes that works. If the other guy can put himself in your shoes and see how annoying the behavior is, sometimes he gets it."

"No...I didn't try that."

"You could try that."

"I suppose so..."

"You want me to talk to her?"

"What? No, I..."

"Because I know her and I think she trusts me. I could talk to her."

My friend was happy, because he was "helping" me with my problem. In point of fact, he wasn't helping at all, but he didn't know that.

Most spiritual directors are keenly aware of their own urge to "fix" and are very careful not to do it. But the more your director cares about you and the closer she feels to you, the harder it will be for her to avoid any kind of "fixing." But hard or not, she knows she is not supposed to do it, and if she is wise and responsible, she won't. You don't need her to solve your problems, after all. You just need her to listen.

SHAMING

Many people equate religion with morality. Sure, there's a connection. Our religious traditions give us tools to help us discern right from wrong. We often have strong traditions about what *is* right and wrong. And let's face it, religious people have been notoriously moralistic throughout history, patting themselves on the back for their own "superior" morality and upbraiding anyone else in the community who didn't measure up to their ethical ideals.

So it's not surprising that some people carry some trepidation into spiritual direction, afraid they're going to be judged by their spiritual director, who, they assume, is much more spiritually advanced and therefore morally superior. But this is nonsense. Your spiritual director shoots milk out of her nose when she laughs, curses her own clumsiness, and messes up royally every single day. Just like I do. Just like you do. Your spiritual director is not necessarily more spiritually advanced than you, nor is she necessarily more "moral" than you. Your spiritual director struggles with her own morality every day. She screws up often. Sometimes she tells people about it, sometimes she doesn't. She's no different from you.

Nor will she act like she's in any way superior to you. In her mind, she's just a fellow traveler privileged to walk beside you for a while. She might be on a pillar in your imagination, but she shouldn't be. She's just as fallible, struggles just as much, and screws up just as often as you do. (She also swears like a longshoreman when she gets a paper cut. I've heard her.)

So you might be afraid that if you reveal your deep dark secrets to her, she might shame you. That might be what you expect from religious people. But she won't. She knows she's a bumbler, and she knows you are too. Your spiritual director will not judge you or condemn you or shame you. Instead, if you are honest with her, I predict that you will be both surprised and relieved at her response to you. Most likely, it will be compassion and understanding and solidarity.

There are few things truly human that will feel alien to her. And even if she might have made different choices were she in the same circumstances, she will most likely understand why you acted as you did. Your secrets are safe with her, and your relationship with her will work best if you are totally, nakedly honest with her. Partly this is because being totally, nakedly honest is the best way to approach the Divine. You might be tempted to be honest with the Divine, but not so honest with your director, but I don't recommend it. The spiritual direction relationship will work best if you can all be on the same page—you, your director, and the Divine.

We all have shame, and shame is a big topic in spiritual direction. The way many religious traditions are taught, we get the idea that the Divine turns away from us because of our guilt, but that is simply not the case. Most often our relationship with the Divine is injured because we turn away from the Divine because of our shame. It is shame, not guilt, that is the problem. It is we who have rejected the Divine, not the Divine who has rejected us. As

Meister Eckhart says, "God is at home, it is we who have gone out for a walk." Working through this shame, discovering our part in it, and healing the relationship with the Divine is part of the important work we come to spiritual direction for.

But if—and that's a very unusual if—your director is unprofessional and does try to shame you, you can simply leave and not go back. Remember that you are always in control here. But that is not likely to happen. Instead, you will most likely find that if you lay out your deepest and darkest secrets, your director will get it. She will have compassion for your journey and your process and your decisions. And she will help you sort through how your decisions have impacted—for good or ill—your relationship with the Divine. And she will help you heal what has been wounded or broken in that relationship. Shame free.

CORRECTING YOUR BELIEFS

Many years ago, I was struggling with many doctrines in my own religious tradition. I knew I needed a spiritual director, but I was afraid to go to a Christian spiritual director for fear that she might try to correct me doctrinally. It is true that, historically, a lot of this kind of thing did indeed go on in spiritual direction. But things have changed. Since the advent of the non-directive method, correcting a client's beliefs is rare.

Spiritual directors are not the thought-police, or, heaven forbid, the religious police. It is not your spiritual director's job to show you where you are in error dogmatically. It is not her job to police your thinking or to eradicate "heresy" when she sees it.

The fact is that because we all have different life experiences, no one believes exactly the same thing—not even very conservative religious people within the same religious community. Everyone has different ideas, and those ideas are colored by what we have seen and experienced. And everyone's beliefs and understandings are always evolving. Always.

Your spiritual director does not assume that her theology is superior to yours, even if your theologies differ greatly. She may consider her theology most appropriate for her, but she will also affirm that where you are right now is exactly where you should be. And that tomorrow, you (and she) will be in a different place.

This does not mean that your director might not point out where your thinking is in-line or out-of-line with a particular orthodoxy—sometimes it's important to know where different communities draw their boundaries of belief. But she will not hold a judgement about whether you are on one side of it or another. And if she has an opinion about it (because we are all human and we all have opinions) she will not let it show. She is a professional, after all. And she knows that you are the expert. She does not know where the Divine is leading you or the route by which you will get there.

Whether a belief or a teaching or a doctrine is fitting for you will always be your decision, not hers. But she will help you examine it, turn it over, think it through. And she may see things you do not, observations which may or may not be helpful. If that sounds like a fine line, it is. But knowing where that line is and staying on the safe side of it is something that spiritual directors are usually pretty good at.

THINGS SPIRITUAL DIRECTORS SAY

*S*piritual direction sessions are completely unpredictable. I often tell my spiritual direction students there's no way to prepare for them because you never know what the Divine is going to do next. This is less true for clients, though. We have already discussed ways that you, as a client, can prepare for a session, but the point is still valid—neither you nor your director will control the flow of the conversation, neither of you know what the Divine is up to, neither of you can have any idea what the session will be like or what wisdom will unfold. It happens in the doing of it.

For all of that, however, there are a few things that spiritual directors often say or do. Let's talk about a few of these, as I think knowing some of them might be helpful. You might not know what the Divine is up to, but you might have a clue what your director is intending.

QUESTIONS

Clarification Questions. By far the most prevalent kind of questions in a spiritual direction session are *clarification questions*. These are questions that arise when your director needs more information to fully understand a situation or a concept or anything else you might be describing. Clarification questions are extremely important in spiritual direction, not only because your director wants (and needs) to fully understand what you are saying, but also for your own clarification. It might seem like an annoying distraction when your director asks you a clarification question, but please be patient with her. She is genuinely interested, the answer is important to her, and there may be information contained within your answer that will be helpful *to you*.

Some examples of clarification questions might be:

- Can you tell me more about the college you went to?
- I don't really understand that doctrine. Can you explain it a bit more?
- So...what were you thinking?
- I've never even heard of Swedenborgianism—what is that?
- Can you tell me more about that?

Clarification questions provide your director with context and texture that help her understand more fully your experience and ideas. Please be patient with her and answer as completely as you can—she means well!

Process Questions. The other most prevalent kinds of questions are what we call process questions. While clarification questions are the kind you probably know the answers to, process questions ask you to dig a little deeper into what might be unfamiliar territory. You may not, in fact, know how to answer the question. You may need to think about it. But more likely, the rooting around and clumsy attempt to explain—before you yourself even understand—is where the real magic is.

Process questions are often the ones that punch us in the gut, the questions that leave us reeling with vertigo, that open new vistas we didn't know existed before. They are often hard questions, even though at first, on the surface, they may seem pedestrian or nonsensical. Your spiritual director is well practiced at asking process questions, and it will soon be clear that this is where her real skill lies.

It's hard to generalize about process questions. They will be very specific to your own case. But just for example, some possible process questions might be:

- If you could go back in time and say anything to the god of your childhood, what would you say?
- What kind of life is worth living?
- If you were the Divine, how would you have handled X (this or that event) differently?
- In what ways do you fall short of your own spiritual ideals? In what ways do you surpass them?
- If the Divine was a piece of music, what would it be and why?

Process questions often ask you to delve into some space you are not familiar with, or at least have not tried to articulate. You may think you know the answer to it, but discover halfway through your explanation that you actually think something else. Process questions help us get to the truth behind our answers, to the "real" us behind our facades. Process questions might be uncomfortable, they might seem invasive or obtuse. But trust your spiritual director and go with it. You might be as surprised to hear what comes out of your mouth as your director is.

"HOW DO YOU FEEL ABOUT THAT?"

A stock question of therapists is also a favorite among spiritual directors. Occupying a no-man's land between clarification and process questioning, "How do you feel about that?" can be a rich source of information, not just for your spiritual director, but for you as well.

Don't roll your eyes when your director says this. It's an important item in her tool kit. This is because feelings are important indicators in discernment. Remember our discussion of St. Ignatius, above? His affective method of discernment tests whether a certain fantasy in prayer elicits a "spirit of consolation" or a "spirit of desolation." When your director asks, "How do you feel about that?" she isn't asking you to engage in full-on Ignatian discernment, but kind of a shorthand version of it. You might be reporting "just the facts, ma'am," to quote Sergeant Friday, but your spiritual director wants to know more than just the facts. She really does want to know how you felt at the time, as well as how you feel now. It may not be immediately obvious why she is asking, or how it can help, but that's okay. Trust the process and trust your spiritual director. There's nothing in your answer that can really hurt you, but it can certainly help.

"LET'S GO BACK TO X…"

So there you are, your conversation is going well. You've been talking for a good forty minutes now, and suddenly there is a lull in the conversation. This happens a lot, and usually your spiritual director just sits there silently, waiting for you to find the thread and continue. But every now and then, she'll step into the silent space and say something like, "Let's go back to when you said…." She will then ask you some follow-up questions, basically resetting the trajectory of the conversation off onto another track.

This is very common, and it can happen for a variety of reasons. It may be that questions arose as you were talking, but she didn't want to interrupt the flow. When a natural break in the conversation occurs, she may naturally want to return to those questions. If your spiritual director takes notes during a session, these "questions to come back to" may be among the things she is writing down as you are talking. They are things she doesn't want to forget, that she wants to explore further once the flow of your current trajectory has run its course.

Another reason your director might ask you to "go back to X" is because you've gotten off-topic, wandered into the weeds or into areas that are simply not in the domain of spiritual direction. Spiritual directors call this "redirection."

There are generally two reasons why people might need some redirection:

First, if you are unfamiliar with spiritual direction, you might not be entirely clear what you are there to talk about, or even if you are, *how* to talk about it. In most of our daily lives, after all, we are actively discouraged from discussing our spiritual lives. Letting go, sinking into the silence, and opening up to another soul about the most intimate details of the most intimate relationship in our life—that doesn't always come easily. Sure, there are those "fire-hose" clients I told you about who are ready and eager, but most of us need a little coaching. You may need to wander in the weeds a bit in order to discover your deep place. You will certainly require a little trial-and-error to get the hang of what is "spiritual direction material" and what is not. Go ahead and wander. When you get too far afield, you can trust that your spiritual director will guide you gently back to safe territory, often by using those magic words: "Let's go back to X..."

Another reason people might not get down to the real meat of things, however, is that they may be actively resisting talking about the deep stuff. This might be conscious or unconscious, but it is most certainly inevitable. Whenever we get close to a profound or painful truth, just before it emerges into consciousness, it seems like everything else in us wants to push it back down where it is "safe" and can't do us any harm. We will often go to great lengths to avoid talking about it. I have had clients who have directly ignored my efforts to direct them back to the matter at hand, and instead have continued to blabber on about "So-and-so said this, and do you think I should repaper my kitchen?" This is a sure-fire sign of resistance, and if your spiritual director is worth her salt, she will not let you get away with it.

This isn't always pleasant, but it is incredibly helpful. Because the very information you are (consciously or unconsciously) trying to keep from emerging into consciousness is healing information, even if it seems scary in the moment when it emerges. And it can sometimes be very scary indeed. When we realize a great truth about ourselves, after all, it means that the illusions are revealed to be just that. This means that we are sometimes robbed of our identities, our self-image, our ideas about ourselves, the world, or even the Divine. This is not comfortable, but it is precisely what we are there for.

Real relationships are based on truth. We must be honest with those we are most intimate with or no real intimacy is possible. This is especially true of the Divine. In order for you to grow into a place of real and deep intimacy with the Divine, you must be honest with it. We can't always do that right away, because we are experts at fooling ourselves as well. But as you and your spiritual director talk, the onion of your soul will be exposed, one layer at a time, and each layer will be more honest, truer, and more real than the last. But peeling that onion will always require some false starts, some wandering in the weeds, and many calls from your director to "Come back to X..."

"WHAT HAPPENS WHEN YOU PRAY ABOUT THAT?"

For theistic clients who pray, this is one of the most predictable responses a spiritual director will give. And yet, strangely, it almost always comes as a surprise. I can't tell you how many times it has happened to me: I'll be telling my spiritual director something that is troubling me, or that I'm struggling with, and then she'll say, "What happens when you pray about that?"

And it stops me cold. Every time. Because pretty much every

time, I *haven't* prayed about it. I've just worried about it. Which means that I've been hoarding it all to myself and not allowing the Divine in on it. This could be for several reasons: I just forgot about it, or I've been resisting praying about it, or I have some unconscious conviction that I *ought* to carry it myself.

But when I do finally pray about it, when I *stop* carrying it all by myself, something shifts. The shift might be subtle or it might be profound, but the shift is always there. Because once it is prayed about, the issue is shared. It is no longer my property or my responsibility alone. I have let the Divine in on it, and it is—at least in part—the Divine's responsibility now, too. And this is all for the good, because now that it's shared, now that it's out in the open, healing and change and transformation can happen around this issue—whatever it is.

And because I say this very same line to all my own clients *all the time*, whenever my spiritual director says it to me, I slap my forehead and feel a brief wave of shame, if not stupidity. Because, you know, I *ought* to know better. And…this happens to all of us. And it's a good, a *necessary* reminder. For those of us who pray, there is nothing that we can't take into prayer.

"WHERE IS THE DIVINE IN THIS?"

We humans have a tendency to compartmentalize our lives—this part is sacred, and this part is mundane. But the whole of our lives —every part of them—are held in the Divine and are part of the Divine life. Your spiritual director may be curious about what the Divine is doing, how the Divine is moving, in parts of your life that you don't normally think of as "spiritual."

For instance, you might think of your spiritual life as some- thing largely interior, something you feel. Most folks will extend this category to include activity in their spiritual communities as well. But your spiritual director will be curious about how the Divine is nudging you and inviting you to growth in your work life, too, in your familial relationships, in your romantic relation-ships and friendships—even in your relationships with your pets.

Spiritual directors use a couple of "maps" to examine all the parts of our lives, such as the Experience Cycle or Ken Wilber's Integral Theory—but there's no need to be so technical. A synthesis of these "maps" invites us to examine how the Divine is active in every possible part of our lives:

- *Our individual interior lives*, including our mind, emotions, our spirit, and the unconscious, including our dreams.
- *Our individual exterior lives*, including our body, our health, money matters, and possessions.
- *Our interior community lives*, including our shared history and culture, our religious and family traditions.
- *Our exterior community lives*, including our relationships and interactions with others, our work and play lives, and our spiritual and social communities.

The Divine is active in all of these arenas, and as you touch on any of these in your session, your spiritual director may be curious about what the Divine is up to, or what the Divine is inviting you to in all of these parts of your life.

"THAT'S OUR TIME"

About five minutes shy of the end of the hour, your director may say, "That's our time." Don't be surprised at this, it's normal. It's not intended to silence you or to be rude. It's simply time. You might have been in the middle of a revelation...but it's time. Part of your success in spiritual direction will be in honoring your boundaries and covenants—this includes boundaries around time.

This is important for your spiritual director because she may have another client waiting to come in at the top of the hour. If your spiritual director sees five people in a day, each at the top of the hour, you can see why she would not want to fall behind—it would not be fair to her other clients. Plus, your director needs time to use the facilities and straighten up before the next client comes in.

"That's our time" will only come as a surprise once. It might be annoying a second time, but you'll soon get the hang of it and anticipate it. One thing that will happen is that you will learn to go deeper, faster, in order to have more time to work. You will learn to shorten the first half where you are "wandering" and debriefing and will get down to the real business of your work together sooner.

Before long, your own internal clock will be set, and you'll find yourself saying to your director, "Well, that's gotta be about our time." Your director will smile when you say that.

WHAT YOUR DIRECTOR WILL EXPECT FROM YOU

*I*n order for your spiritual direction session to run smoothly, and to get the most done in the small amount of time you have together, your spiritual director will expect certain things of you. In this chapter, we'll talk about those things, since many times these "expectations" go unsaid. Since your spiritual director has probably been doing this a long time and often works with clients who have also been at it for quite a while, she might forget what it's like to be a "newbie" and will forget that you don't know all the rules or the secret handshake. (That was a joke. There is no secret handshake. In case you were wondering.)

COME PREPARED TO YOUR SESSION

Your time is valuable—and so is your director's. Yes, it's true, you will probably be paying your director for her time, but she will still want to use that time productively. Just how productive your time will be will often be determined by how prepared you are when you come in for a session.

Of course, you can never be prepared for what happens *in a* session—that is always gift and surprise. It is never something you can predict or plan out. But your session will be much more productive if you have given some thought to your session beforehand.

That might mean going over the list you've been making for the past month of things you want to talk about in your session, and picking out the one or two items that have the most energy for you.

It might mean praying about your session before you go in, sitting silent before the Divine and asking for help discerning the most important topics to discuss, and asking that your session be blessed and fruitful.

It might mean taking ten minutes after arriving but before going in to center yourself and meditate. (This requires planning!)

After some trial and error, you'll have a good sense of what good preparation looks like *for you*. However you do it, this expectation is about mindfulness—about taking your session seriously, and making sure that you are in the best place to get the most out of it.

CARRY THE WEIGHT IN THE SESSION

Your session is *your session*—it's your dime and your time. If you show up and just sit there, not speaking or making any effort, your director is perfectly within her rights to simply sit there with you. She might think what you need is silence, and she will be happy to share that silence with you. Or she might sense that something is amiss and ask you about it. The point is that it's not your spiritual director's job to keep the conversation going in the spiritual direction session. It's not *about* conversation, really, but companionship. So if you don't speak, there could be a lot of silence. Your spiritual director will be comfortable with silence, but will you be?

Maybe so. Maybe your soul is thirsty for silence in the presence of another. If so, this is a good and productive use of your time together.

If you have arrived at the session unprepared (see above), you could find yourself stumbling around, looking for something to talk about, and passing your valuable time away with filler that doesn't really pertain to your spiritual life as such.

But if you have prepared, then you will know deep in your heart of hearts what needs to be shared that day. You will know what it is within you that needs to be witnessed. You will know the questions that cry out for answers. You will feel the longing for your secret name, and that longing will pull you on, even if you can't exactly see the path.

The most important thing to remember, however, is that this time is yours, and whether it is a useful and productive time or not lies squarely on your shoulders. Your spiritual director is available to you, with every scrap of attention that she can muster on that particular day. But she does not know your soul, does not know what it is within you that most needs expression. She does not know what your soul has been wrestling with, or what is tripping you up with your spiritual practice. You must tell her. Only you can "bring it."

IF YOU MISS AN APPOINTMENT

What happens if you have a flat tire on your way to a session? That—or something very like that—has happened to all of us. Your spiritual director will understand completely and will not hold it against you—so long as you let her know. When something unforeseen strikes, just give your spiritual director a call or shoot her a text. "Got a flat tire—gotta reschedule" is a short text message, but will do the job handily. That lets your spiritual director know that you can't make it, why you can't make it, and that you'll be in touch soon to get another appointment on the calendar. Easy!

Sometimes you have a bit more warning, though, and more warning is good. Let's say your session is tomorrow and you come down with a nasty cold today. You can be pretty sure that you will not be going out to infect the wider world tomorrow, so a call or a text to your spiritual director ahead of time is a good idea.

Your spiritual director will appreciate a 24-hour warning if you find you will not be able to make a session. You can't foresee a flat tire or a car accident or many other unexpected events—your spiritual director will forgive those—but there are lots of other situations where you *do* know ahead of time you won't be able to make it. Please make sure you let your spiritual director know.

If you must cancel, the standard practice is to give your spiritual director 24 hours' notice—flat tires, illness, and other unavoidable situations excepted. If you do not, you are still financially responsible for the session.

This is especially true of those times when you have forgotten about the session or forgot to enter it into your calendar and simply don't show up. Again, this happens to the best of us now and then, and the best of us take responsibility for it and pay our spiritual directors for that time anyway.

Usually, your spiritual director will give you one "pass" the first time this happens, with a gentle warning that the next time it happens, you will need to pay for the missed time. This is only fair, since your spiritual director could have used the missed appointment time for another client or other productive activities. If spiritual direction is part of how your director earns her living, it is especially important to honor her time, and to compensate her for her lost earnings.

All this talk of payment brings us to a discussion of…

COMPENSATION

Compensation is a sensitive subject in the spiritual direction community. As I've already mentioned above, some spiritual directors consider their practice a gift to the world and do not charge for it. Most, however, charge a fair rate for their time. There is nothing shameful about this—believe me, *no one* is getting rich doing spiritual direction. In fact, because spiritual directors charge far less than other helping professions (such as therapists) it is difficult to make a living doing spiritual direction, even full time. (There are those who do, but not many. Those who do often make barely enough to squeak by.)

Spiritual direction is a professional ministry—which is a good thing, because it means you can expect a high level of quality and professionalism. It requires expensive training and ongoing attention to education and supervision. Sometimes, it requires leasing a professional office. Your spiritual director is worthy of her wage. Her time is valuable—to her, certainly, but also to you. In North American and European cultures, we don't tend to value things we don't pay for. Paying for spiritual direction sends a message, both to you and to your spiritual director that says, "I'm serious about this. I'm so serious I'm willing to pay for it. Here is my proof."

Exactly how much will your spiritual director charge for her time? That depends on a lot of factors. Here are a few of them:

Location. Where the cost of living is high, the cost of spiritual direction will be higher, too. For instance, if you live near New York or Chicago or San Francisco or Los Angeles, you can expect to pay anywhere between $50 and $150 per session. However, if you live in a rural area, you might expect to pay between $25 and $50 per session.

Experience. If your spiritual director is a student or an intern, she probably won't be allowed to charge for her services—most training programs require students/interns to work gratis. Once your student director graduates, however, she will start charging for her time, on the low end of the scale. As she gains skill and experience (and a reputation for excellence) she will eventually charge more for her time. Near San Francisco, where I live, a novice spiritual director usually charges between $40 and $50 per session. A very experienced spiritual director may charge between $75 and $125 per session. In a rural area, this will be less—a novice may charge $25 per session, while an experienced director might charge $50.

Private Practice vs. Institution. If your director is in private practice, she will set her own fees and can change them at any time. If you go to an institution for spiritual direction—such as a convent or a retreat center—the institution will set the fee (or more likely, for legal reasons, the "suggested donation").

Flexibility. How flexible will your spiritual director be on her fee? That depends upon your spiritual director. Many spiritual directors work on a sliding scale. Many will have different rates for working people and students. And some will say, "This is my livelihood, and I need to make $X per session to survive" and so will not offer a sliding scale or any flexibility. That is her right! Even if your spiritual director does not offer a sliding scale, however, and after many years of working together you suddenly lose your job, most directors will work with you to find a reasonable compromise until you get on your feet again.

WHAT YOU CAN EXPECT FROM YOUR DIRECTOR

*I*n order to do good work in spiritual direction, you must feel safe. Spiritual directors around the world have agreed on a simple statement of ethical principles that we all agree to uphold: *The Spiritual Directors International Guidelines for Ethical Conduct.* Knowing what these principles are can go a long way to providing a sense of security. If you have any doubts about whether your spiritual director subscribes to these guidelines, just ask. Also, if you ever have any doubts about whether your director is acting according to the guidelines, don't hesitate to remind her about them, and tell her you expect her to uphold them. If she is a worthy spiritual director, she will agree with you 100% and will be eager to reassure you of her adherence to these rules.

You can read the Guidelines in full in the Appendix, but for the rest of this chapter, we'll focus on each of the main points so that you will have a clear sense of what you can expect from your director.

The following falls into the category
of your director's care for herself:

YOUR DIRECTOR HAS RECEIVED ADEQUATE TRAINING

This is not part of the guidelines—probably because it was unthinkable to the drafters that anyone would practice spiritual direction without proper training. As we have discussed, it is not illegal to do so, but it is unethical. Part of your director's commitment to herself is proper training—which is to say, completing a reputable training program. There is no licensing body, so directors do not hold licenses. They hold certificates of completion from training programs. Ask your director to show you her certificate of completion. It's probably already there on the wall, framed. But if not, feel free to ask. *Please make sure your director is a graduate of a reputable program before you proceed with her.*

YOUR DIRECTOR IS WORKING ON HER OWN SPIRITUAL LIFE

It isn't enough for her to have training. Your spiritual director must also be a person who is practicing what she preaches. She must be working on her own spiritual life with as much diligence as you are working on yours. It is an unspoken covenant, usually, but it is certainly implied by the spiritual direction relationship. You wouldn't buy a car from someone who doesn't drive. You wouldn't take skiing lessons from someone who doesn't know how to ski. Just so, you don't want spiritual direction from someone who is not committed to her own spiritual path and progress.

This means that your spiritual director is also in spiritual direction. That's right, your spiritual director has a spiritual director. It is, in fact, unethical for her to offer you spiritual direction if she is not receiving spiritual direction from someone else.

Your spiritual director is also committed to being in spiritual community, and has a dedicated spiritual practice. That practice may look very different from yours, and it might change and evolve as time goes on—that's all well and good. You would want and expect that—a spirituality that isn't growing and evolving is a dead spirituality after all. What is important is that your spiritual director isn't asking anything of you that she herself hasn't committed to. She is committed to her own spiritual practice.

YOUR DIRECTOR IS COMMITTED TO CONTINUING HER EDUCATION

Just as you never stop learning, your spiritual director is committed to being a "lifelong learner" in her craft of spiritual guidance as well. This means that she is not only committed to her own ongoing spiritual growth and to discerning how her own call might be evolving, she is also attempting to stay current on the latest thinking in spiritual direction, learning from her own ongoing experience and from the experience of her peers.

She does this in many ways: Through the reading of scripture —of her own tradition and perhaps others, gleaning insights for spiritual guidance. She reads about spirituality and spiritual development, always looking for that surprise or that "aha" that is going to provide a spiritual breakthrough for her or for one of her clients—perhaps even you. She may even read about other helping professions, such as pastoral counseling or transpersonal psychology, looking for ways to grow and deepen in her practice.

She will read farther afield as well, trying to get a grasp on the current cultural milieu. She will see movies that people are likely to be discussing and read novels and non-fiction that are making an impact on the culture. She knows she won't serve you well if she's living in a cave—so she tries to keep her finger on the pulse of the culture you share.

More specifically to the practice of spiritual direction, she will read *Presence*, the international journal of spiritual direction published by Spiritual Directors International. She will read new books on the practice of spiritual direction and may discuss these with other directors in her peer supervision group.

She will probably attend local gatherings of spiritual directors. At these meetings, spiritual directors network with each other, discover one another's specialties, and usually hear a lecture from someone in their field. She may go to workshops or classes or conferences. Spiritual Directors International holds an annual conference every year that combines all of these activities: networking, news, lectures, and classes. Attending the annual SDI conference is a great way for your spiritual director to continue her education. Many hundreds of directors attend every year.

YOUR DIRECTOR PARTICIPATES IN SUPERVISION

Not only does your spiritual director see a spiritual director of her own, but she also has a supervisor. This might seem like overkill, but it really isn't. Her spiritual direction session is where she works on her own spiritual life, but her supervision session is where she works on issues that arise from her spiritual direction practice.

A spiritual direction supervisor has special training and is an expert at helping your spiritual director navigate some of the trickier aspects of her practice. Her supervisor will help her unpack what the Divine might be up to in the sessions, both for you as a client and for her as the director as well. (No names are used in a supervision session, so while the content of a spiritual direction session might be discussed, it remains completely anonymous.)

In a normal supervisory session, your director may talk about an issue that is arising with one of her clients. (Don't automatically assume she's talking about you—that will probably happen at some point in your relationship, but you'll never know, and there's no reason you should.) Often these are questions where your director is trying to discern a good boundary, or wondering whether a response she gave to someone was appropriate. Almost always, however, the supervisory conversation ends up with a discernment about what the Divine might be saying to your spiritual director through this encounter with her client. If you think that sounds like more spiritual direction...well, it kind of is.

Your director's supervisor might be a person with special training, but your director might also attend a peer supervision group as well. In such groups, the collective wisdom of a small group of directors—some of them new, some of them seasoned—tends to the supervisory task. Such groups usually meet once a month, and members take turns presenting a case from their practice—usually one or two cases per meeting. Even if your director doesn't present at a group meeting, she learns from the experience of her colleagues, and vice versa.

When your spiritual director has been seeing clients for five years or more, she might discern whether the Divine is calling her to be a supervisor herself. Mentoring younger spiritual directors in the art is part of our responsibility to the community. She might then go and do the supplemental training necessary to become a supervisor. You probably won't know if your spiritual director is a supervisor or not, unless you ask. If she is, she will most likely have some clients who are there for spiritual direction and some who are there for supervision.

Supervision is essential for good spiritual direction. You would do well to inquire as to whether your spiritual director is seeing a supervisor or is involved in a supervisory group. If not, you should find another spiritual director. Supervision provides invaluable opportunities for discernment and accountability that all spiritual directors need. Being involved in supervision isn't just a good idea, it is an ethical necessity.

JOHN R. MABRY

YOUR DIRECTOR TAKES CARE OF HERSELF

Your director can't be of much use to you if she isn't taking care of herself. Self-care is a big issue for people in ministry, which makes sense. People who have dedicated their lives to helping others often don't know where to stop, and they can become depleted and burn out. Your director will not be immune to this temptation, but if she is wise, she will strive to overcome it and practice being self-ish in a good way—caring enough for herself and her needs so that she can be the most available and useful to others.

She does this by finding just the right balance between work, family, and personal time. This last is often the place where people get into trouble, so a responsible spiritual director makes sure she has time for play, reflection, rest, and spiritual practice.

She also takes care of herself by maintaining good boundaries between herself and...well, you. Spiritual direction is a professional relationship. It might seem strange that you share the most intimate details of your inner life with this person, but then she doesn't want to see you outside of the direction session. Don't be hurt, she's just doing her job. Just as psychotherapists aren't allowed to see their clients socially, just so spiritual directors aren't either. Many difficulties can arise from "dual relationships"—they start out innocently enough, but as many spiritual directors have discovered to their great peril, they can get very sticky and thorny very quickly. For this reason, spiritual directors who practice ethically do not have their friends or relatives as clients, nor do they socialize outside the session with their clients.

Your director might be a member of your spiritual community —this is very common. You may see her at worship, you might wash dishes together after coffee hour, you might serve on a committee together. But if you ask her and her spouse over for

68

dinner, she will say "no." Don't be offended—she has to say this. She must maintain good boundaries to serve you well.

If you and she find yourselves in a situation where you must spend more time together—let's say the activity on that committee really ramps up—your director will probably tap you on the shoulder and suggest that she give you a referral to another spiritual director. This is a good idea. You might really like her and feel you are getting good value from your spiritual direction relationship, but please honor her need to keep personal and professional separate, and take the referral with grace. Your director is not the only person who can do a good job for you. You may discover a great fit with your new director, too.

Your director also takes care of herself by knowing where her limits are. She makes sure she doesn't take on too many clients and doesn't try to pack too many clients into one day. For myself, I know that after four back-to-back clients, I'm pretty tired. A fifth client would not get the best "me" possible, so I never schedule more than four clients in a day. Other people have different limits, but knowing what their limit *is* is an essential skill for directors. Also, making sure there's enough space between clients to clear one's head and use the facilities is important, too.

There are other important limits, as well. Perhaps your director is easily triggered by clients of one tradition or another. For instance, if your director suffered as a child from an abusive form of religion, it might be that she cannot see clients from that particular religion. This is not a failure. Knowing who you can and can't work with is part of being a good director. Some directors work only with people from their own spiritual tradition or from one family of traditions, while others work with people of many different traditions. Just as you get to choose your director, your director gets to choose whom she will work with, based on her own discernment about whom she can direct responsibly and well.

The following falls into the category
of your director's care for you:

YOUR DIRECTOR WILL BE CLEAR WITH YOU ABOUT HER COVENANT WITH YOU

In your first session or so, your spiritual director will most likely make sure you are on the same page about her understanding of spiritual direction. As we discussed above, she might initiate that conversation by asking what *you* think you're supposed to be doing in direction. As you both explain your understandings, you will be able to negotiate an agreement about the scope and nature of your work together. At the very least, it is your director's responsibility to make clear to you her own understanding of what spiritual direction is for and how you will go about it.

This includes defining your respective roles as client and director. This will probably include a lot of what we have already discussed regarding what your director expects from you and what you can expect from her. She might talk about boundaries, and about which kinds of things you will—and won't —talk about.

Your director will make sure that you're on the same page about other things, too, such as the length of your sessions and how often you will see each other. You should never agree to spiritual direction sessions that go for more than an hour. One hour is more than enough time for anything you will need to say or process. Any longer will begin to feel like an endurance test. Likewise, sessions that are much shorter than an hour won't be of much use, either. Many directors (myself included) do a "50-minute hour" so that they can see clients on the hour. This sometimes leads to a rushed end-of-session. But so long as your director is clear with you about both the length of your session as well as her expectations for handling the end of an intense session, you'll soon get the hang of it. Don't be surprised when your director says, "That's our time," and expects you to do your scheduling and parting efficiently. That's the deal!

How often will you and your director meet? You should be on the same page about that, too. Normally, spiritual directors see their clients once a month. If you are new to spiritual direction and have a lot to process, or if you are going through a particularly intense discernment, you might want to see her twice a month for a while. But once through that phase, she will probably recommend that you go back to once per month. This is a good idea.

In my experience, people who feel like they "need" to see their spiritual director more than once a month are misguided—what they probably need is psychotherapy rather than spiritual direction. This is not a judgment, and please don't read it that way—it is simply a fact. Spiritual direction should never become a *dependent* relationship. Spiritual direction is helpful, but you should never consider it essential to life. If you discover you "need" to see your spiritual director more and more often, please exercise some good self-care and make sure you are also seeing a competent therapist. Otherwise your director may need to set a boundary with you, or may even need to terminate the relationship. Usually, however, directors can successfully negotiate an arrangement with their clients so that they can both get the therapy they need and continue with spiritual direction.

Finally, you and your director should spend a little time discussing how you will assess your time together. Often, directors will check in once per year to ask, "How did we do this year? Is this work bearing fruit? Where would you like to be in a year?" These can be very good conversations, and can both redirect and energize the direction relationship. It might also be helpful in discerning when a relationship should come to a natural end, or when working with a new spiritual director might be helpful.

And speaking of ends, this too should be spoken of at the beginning of your relationship: is your work together for a specific period of time (three months? six months?) or is it open-ended? Most direction relationships are open ended, but sometimes people want to work on specific discernments and will request to work with a director for a specified number of sessions or length of time. Both are normal, and setting a time limit for an evaluation can be a very helpful tool indeed.

Instead of spending time in your first session covering these items, sometimes a spiritual director will have all of these expectations spelled out in writing. She might give you a copy of this "covenant" or "contract" and ask you to take it home after your first session and bring a signed copy back with you for your second session. This, too, is normal, and can be very useful. You will know, in writing and up front, what your director's commitments to you are, as well as what she expects from you. You will both have clarity about those expectations, and it will save session time for whatever *you* want to talk about. Of course, in such a situation, feel free to ask for clarifications or negotiate specific points when you bring the covenant back on your second session. Working through the covenant might provide a great starting point for a session, in fact, if there is not a more pressing discernment.

YOUR DIRECTOR WILL GUARD YOUR DIGNITY

Spiritual direction is truly safe space, and your director takes this very seriously. She won't impose her own beliefs on you or expect you to believe exactly what she does. She will respect your beliefs and the ways that you hold your faith—even if that faith (or the way that you hold it) is very different from her own. If you feel concerned about that, please let me assure you that an experienced spiritual director has been around the block a few times—she has had many clients whose beliefs differed from her own, and she has probably worked through whatever issues she might have had with that. In fact, many training centers emphasize this kind of spiritual diversity. If her classmates held very different beliefs from her own, then she has had good practice right from the beginning. Feel free to ask her about her training or the diversity of her other clients. Don't be afraid to talk about your fears! You won't hurt her feelings and she can put you at ease quickly.

Your spiritual director will honor your privacy in other areas of your life. In your spiritual life, okay, she's going to be nosy—that's her job. But in the other arenas of your life—your relationships, your history, your work life—she will only inquire into these to the extent that they have bearing on your relationship with the Divine. You can always tell her, "I'm not comfortable talking about that," if she gets close to a subject that feels too private or scary. She may poke at the edges to be sure that this is not related to your spirituality in any way, but once she understands that it isn't, she will set it aside. She might suggest you take something up with your therapist—that's okay, because that is the appropriate arena of therapy.

Your spiritual director will guard your dignity by never losing sight of the fact that you are coming to her for assistance, and there is an implied imbalance of power in that arrangement. That imbalance of power is largely an illusion, but it certainly feels real. In reality, though, your spiritual director has no power over you: you are always in control of what you share, of what happens in a session, or whether you will come back for another session. There is nothing your spiritual director will do (if she is reputable and responsible) that will negatively impact your life. You are always in charge of whether to accept an interpretation of a dream, or whether to pursue a spiritual practice, or whether to embrace a belief. Your spiritual director has no real power over you.

You should always refuse to work with a spiritual director who does have any real power over you. You should never see one of your teachers for spiritual direction (if that teacher has any role in evaluating your grade, that is). You should never see your rabbi or pastor or roshi for spiritual direction—you may consult them on religious matters and ask them for spiritual guidance, but the ongoing relationship of spiritual direction is a different thing, and it should be kept separate from other important relationships in your life—especially from any kind of relationship where there is a power imbalance or a dual relationship.

Your spiritual director will help in this, too. She knows that there is, somewhere in your imagination, a perceived power imbalance, and she is committed to avoiding even the appearance of exploiting that difference. If she perceives that you have her on some kind of pedestal, she will generally address that and assure you that she is as clay-footed as the next screw-up. I usually knock over that pillar by cussing a blue streak—but your director may have less dramatic ways of going about it.

Your director will guard your dignity by setting and maintaining good boundaries with you. Good boundaries are so important in spiritual direction, because the work can be intense and you don't want any other relationships between you and your director to color or influence or even "infect" the work. This is why you should not see a spiritual director that you have any other kind of relationship with. You should not see someone you socialize with, for instance. A total stranger, who remains a total stranger (except when you are in your session) is best.

That said, it is not your job to maintain those good boundaries —you are the client, not the professional. It is your spiritual director's job to hold good boundaries. So please don't be upset when your spiritual director sets a boundary with you. It's nothing personal, but it is for her protection and yours. And she knows a lot more about where the tricky (and often unseen) boundary issues are in spiritual direction—so expect her to surprise you now and then with a boundary that you didn't see coming, and take it in stride. Before long you'll probably see why it was a good idea and will be grateful for it.

Just a short example: I had a client who brought me a Christmas gift. If it had been an inexpensive gift of cookies, I would have accepted it with thanks, but it was a much more extravagant gift. I told her that I would not be able to accept such a gift, although I was touched by her generosity. She was hurt at first, but when I explained that some clients might expect something in return for such gifts, she understood why I could not, in good conscience, accept it. It did create some tension between us for a while, however, so it is best to avoid such incidents when you can.

There are many boundary issues your director will be watching out for. She will want to make sure there is appropriate distance between you, so that you don't feel crowded or experience any unwanted or uncomfortable intimacy between you. She will also hold psychological boundaries, making sure that your relationship does not slide into dependence or some kind of twisted space where you feel beholden to her or obligated to be obedient in any way. She will also hold a strong boundary against any kind of emotional attachment or sexual behavior.

This is especially important because, as you bare your soul in spiritual direction, you might discover that your director is one of the few people in the world who really "gets" you. The level of intimacy between you might naturally lead you to think of intimacy in other ways. This is especially dangerous ground if you are physically attracted to your spiritual director.

Allow me to put you at ease: this happens all the time, and you should feel no shame if you find yourself attracted to your spiritual director, or even if you find that you have feelings for her. This is perfectly natural, and it happens to many of us. Those feelings may be uncomfortable, but it is not wrong to have them. Acting on those feelings, however, is very wrong—not for you, necessarily, but for your spiritual director. Again, it is not wrong to have such feelings, or even to voice them. But you must not expect your spiritual director to reciprocate or to act on them— even if she shares them. As a professional, it is her job to protect herself and you by keeping a strong and absolute boundary between the two of you, and to maintain the direction relationship you have covenanted for.

If something like this happens, don't despair, because there is much good news in this. Adolescents might be buffeted by emotional winds beyond their control, but adults should keep in mind that feelings are ephemeral—they rise and fall like waves on the ocean. Feelings of lust or infatuation are a form of temporary insanity caused by naturally occurring drugs produced by your own body. Drugs wear off, and so will the limerence you feel. It might be uncomfortable, but if you ride it out I promise you it will pass. I speak from many long years of experience!

If you choose to reveal your feelings to your director, it would be wise not to expect her to feel the same way and be ready to run away together. She will probably tell you she is flattered, but that her relationship with you is strictly professional, and that a romance between you will never happen. She will say this kindly but firmly. She will then probably ask you to discern whether, given your feelings and your disappointment, you will be able to continue working together. This is a good question, and if your feelings are especially intense, it might be wise to take a referral to another spiritual director. This will be someone your director knows and trusts, and even if it is only a temporary arrangement, it is probably a good idea. You can talk through your feelings with your therapist, of course—also a good idea.

Your spiritual director isn't trying to hurt you. She is just trying to stay safe—and to keep you safe, too. She is bound by her covenant with you and with other spiritual directors not to behave toward you in a way that is sexual or manipulative or abusive. It is her responsibility to ensure that spiritual direction is safe space—for you and for her.

YOUR DIRECTOR WILL RESPECT YOUR CONFIDENTIALITY

One of the most important aspects of spiritual direction is confidentiality. With few exceptions (which we will talk about) anything you say in the spiritual direction session *stays* in the spiritual direction session. This is important, because often we are sharing some of the deepest and most intimate details of our lives. You need to be able to trust your spiritual director absolutely. And if your director is reputable, ethical, and responsible, you can. If you are part of the same spiritual community, you don't need to worry about content from your session "leaking" into the community. However, as a safeguard, this is one argument for picking a spiritual director who is *not* part of your spiritual community.

But what about those exceptions? We have already discussed one of them: supervision. Your spiritual director will be discussing the content of your session with her supervisor or supervisory group. This is standard practice in most helping professions. It is a desirable thing both for your director and for you, since supervision provides your director with both a reality check and accountability. If your director is ever off base in her response to you, her supervisor or group will let her know that, and she will tailor her future responses accordingly. She will not share willy-nilly with her supervisor or group—she may divulge content from the session, but never your identity. She will choose a different name for you and may change your gender before presenting the case. Be assured that her supervisor is under the same strict confidentiality rules as your director is, and *it stops there*. Might a supervisor take an issue to *her* supervisor? Perhaps, but it's rare.

If your director takes notes on your session (and she should, whether during a session or immediately after it) her covenant of confidentiality with you demands that she keep those notes in a secure place, where no one else can discover or read them. One thing to keep in mind: If your director is in private practice, the notes belong to her. If your director works for an institution, like a retreat center, the notes are work product and are the property of the retreat center. This means that, in theory at least, your director's employer has access to her notes. However, in actual practice I have never heard of a director turning her notes over to anyone. In the case of a criminal trial, her notes may theoretically be subpoenaed, but your director does not have to surrender them. Again, I have never heard of a case where this has happened.

The most important thing to remember is that the content of your session will be held in the strictest confidence—not secrecy, but confidence. This may manifest itself in unexpected ways. If you see your spiritual director on the street walking with her husband, she may make eye contact with you and smile but she will not say "hello." She isn't being cold or callous—she's respecting your confidentiality. Feel free to say, "Hey, Meg! Great to see you! Who's your guy?" But it will be *you* choosing to let her husband in on the fact that she is your director—she will not betray this herself.

Your director also respects your confidentiality by making sure you are meeting in a secure space, where no one else can hear. If you are meeting in a busy office building, this might mean she puts a white noise generator outside her door to make sure that no one can hear what you say. (I am certain that no one in the building I work in can hear my clients when they are talking normally, but when they scream expletives—which happens more often than you might think—I do wonder about what the preschool teachers next door think!)

The biggest exception to confidentiality is one to which all helping professionals must submit themselves—being a mandated reporter. Your spiritual director is a mandated reporter— everyone in the ministry agrees with this, every bit as much as an ordained minister or a licensed psychotherapist. There are no exceptions. This means that if your spiritual director hears anything in her sessions indicating child abuse or elder abuse or dependent adult abuse she must report it to law enforcement authorities, immediately and without fail. To fail to do so would put her on the wrong side of the law.

What constitutes abuse? Details differ from state to state, but generally, abuse is understood to mean physical injury, sexual abuse, willful cruelty or unjustified punishment, unlawful corporal punishment or injury, and neglect. Your spiritual director must also report if a client indicates a desire to harm anyone (including herself).

These are extreme interventions, and your spiritual director will not take them lightly. Fortunately, few spiritual directors ever have to act on them. The exception to this is when a client mentions the possibility of suicide, which is quite common. Everyone feels despair now and then, and most spiritual directors know that "suicide talk" is just that: talk. But some people actually go through with it. In this case, spiritual directors need to make a judgment call. If a director's gut tells her that the client is serious and will most likely act on the threat, she will need to report it. If her gut tells her that the client is just talking through his options and isn't likely to act, then she probably will not report it— although she may require the client to see a therapist and/or to make a covenant with the director to call before doing anything "rash."

As you might expect, no spiritual director wants the death of a client on their conscience, and some spiritual directors in that position may be more cautious than others. All spiritual directors take these matters seriously and are fully aware of their responsibilities—both to their clients and to society at large.

The following falls into the category
of your director's care for her colleagues:

YOUR DIRECTOR WILL RESPECT HER COLLEAGUES

Your spiritual director has great respect not only for her fellow spiritual directors (with whom she is in community and networks with regularly) but also therapists, clergy, and other helping professionals. It is very likely that she has friends in these fields, discusses aspects of her practice with them (though not the details of her clients' lives), and sometimes seeks their advice.

To show this respect, she may ask you to inform your therapist (or other helping professional you might be working with) that you are in spiritual direction. If she feels it would be beneficial to you to talk to your therapist or other professional—and if you agree—she may ask you to sign a release, allowing her to speak freely to the other helping professional about your case.

Part of your director's ethical practice is her respect and support for these other professionals, and she will be careful not to criticize them in your hearing.

YOUR DIRECTOR WILL RESPECT BOTH HER OWN FAITH AND YOURS

If your director is acting ethically and responsibly, she won't criticize your beliefs or try to change them. In fact, she will most likely listen very closely to the way that you speak about the Divine, and will use your own images, metaphors, names, and concepts in speaking to you. She may use a story or an example from her own faith tradition, but it will only be by way of illustration, not because she thinks you should believe like she does.

However, your director may have a strong bias toward spiritual community, and if you are not part of a spiritual community, you can expect her to press you on this point until you join one. This isn't about not respecting your beliefs, it's just that she knows something about the spiritual journey and the process of spiritual development—we need others to do this well. It is primarily in community that we receive the lion's share of support for our spiritual journeys, avail ourselves of group discernment, and are held accountable by our peers—all good and important and even necessary aspects of spiritual life. Community really is the crucible in which a soul is forged. A solitary spirituality is prone to narcissism, self-involvement, and even self-delusion. Community life slaps that nonsense right out of you the moment you are challenged to actively and truly love someone you can't stand and don't want to be around. Nothing grows a soul faster!

Because of this you can expect your spiritual director to have a great deal of respect for your spiritual community. She will be very interested in the discernments you are making together, and the ways your community supports and challenges and stretches you in both delightful and uncomfortable ways.

If your director is familiar with your faith tradition, you can expect her to "draw from its well," offering examples and suggesting practices that will be familiar to you and your faith community. And just as a DJ might delight radio listeners with a "deep cut," an album track that never made the Top 40, your director may surprise you with a concept or practice from your community's deep history that is not particularly well-known today.

All of this is to say that your director will respect your faith and your spiritual community, and will encourage you to be deeply involved with it, encouraging you to allow it to form and inform you. She knows that your spiritual community is the best spiritual director you will ever have. She plays a support role to this most important aspect of your spiritual life.

JOHN R. MABRY

YOUR DIRECTOR WILL PRESENT HERSELF AS AN HONORABLE PERSON IN SOCIETY

Another way your director shows respect for her colleagues is by not behaving in a way that will bring shame to the ministry—even in her private life when she is "off duty." She doesn't misrepresent herself, claiming degrees or qualifications she doesn't possess. She is honest and forthright about her training, her affiliations, and her accomplishments. In speaking about spiritual direction, she is clear about what the ministry is and what it isn't, and she doesn't try to practice therapy under another guise.

Your director guards her honor and the honor of her profession by treating all people with respect and dignity, including people of all nationalities and ethnicities and cultures and skin colors, people of all sexes, sexual orientations, and gender designations, people of all ages, married or partnered, unmarried or unpartnered or divorced, people of all political persuasions, people both able and handicapped. In other words, she treats all people with dignity and honor, without exception.

IDEALS AND REALITY

When we are talking about ethics we are talking about ideals and aspirations. Will your spiritual director do all these things perfectly? No. But your spiritual director strives for her highest spiritual and ethical ideals, just as you do. She, too, has her blind spots and is working through them. But a responsible and ethical spiritual director will agree with the ethical guidelines set out by Spiritual Directors International (which is what we've been summarizing and discussing) and will strive to embody them in her own life.

Every now and then you might feel like your spiritual director has crossed a line into territory you feel is inappropriate or that makes you uncomfortable. It is perfectly permissible to bring this up with your spiritual director—she might even thank you for bringing it to her attention.

No one is perfect, and spiritual direction doesn't demand perfection from anyone, even from spiritual directors. We are all human and we all make mistakes. We are also always learning and growing. Perfection does not exist anywhere in the phenomenal universe except in the human imagination—mostly as a stick we use to beat up on ourselves and others.

If we only let perfect people do ministry, we wouldn't have any ministers and no ministry would get done, because there are no perfect people. There are only messy people bumbling their way through life, doing the best they can. Your spiritual director is one of those. When she trips up, remember to show her the same patience and grace that she has shown you. I guarantee you that she is learning as much from your sessions as you are, and like you, she is also a work in progress.

That being said, if your director behaves in an unethical way, you are under no obligation to stay. Once again, you are always in control. If you ever feel uncomfortable or feel that you have been violated in any way, you may simply get up and walk out. If you feel that it's important to offer an explanation, you may call or email your director later, but there is no obligation to do so. It might benefit your director and her future clients, however, to know how her words or behavior impacted you.

These experiences, however, are rare—you will find the vast majority of spiritual directors to be well-trained, self-aware, deeply respectful of your faith, and protective of your soul.

AFTERWORD

Spiritual direction isn't a cure-all or a one-size-fits-all answer to your spiritual problems. But it is a great adventure that can support you, help you stay focused on your spiritual practice, and help you grow in ways that will delight and surprise and challenge you. It is a ministry of accompaniment, of hospitality, and of mindful attention. It doesn't work quickly, but slowly, over many years. It doesn't change us, but sustains us through a process of transformation in both our inner and outer lives. Spiritual direction doesn't give us any answers, but it holds us and encourages us as we ask all the right questions, questions that cut to the heart of who we are, what we are here for, and what—in our heart of hearts—we are called to be. Spiritual direction is not a destination, but a journey.

That is not a journey for the faint of heart. That's why we don't walk the path alone, but with another, one who respects us and prays for and with us, one for whom our spiritual flourishing is the number-one priority.

Welcome to the journey.

APPENDIX A

SPIRITUAL DIRECTORS INTERNATIONAL GUIDELINES FOR ETHICAL CONDUCT

Ethical conduct flows from lived reverence for Divinity, self, and others but is not inevitably the reality of every spiritual direction relationship. Therefore, these guidelines are meant to inspire members of Spiritual Directors International toward integrity, responsibility, and faithfulness in their practice of spiritual direction.

I. THE SPIRITUAL DIRECTOR AND THE SELF

1. Personal Spirituality. Spiritual directors assume responsibility for personal growth by: a) participating in regular spiritual direction; b) following personal and communal spiritual practices and disciplines.

2. Formation. Spiritual directors engage in ongoing formation as directors by: a) continuing to discern their call to the ministry of spiritual direction; b) nurturing self-knowledge and freedom; c) cultivating insight into the influences of culture, social-historical context, environmental setting, and institutions; d) studying scripture, theology, spirituality, and other disciplines related to spiritual direction.

3. Supervision. Spiritual directors engage in supervision by a) receiving regular supervision from peers or from a mentor; b) seeking consultations with other appropriately qualified persons when necessary.

4. Personal Responsibility. Spiritual directors meet their needs outside the spiritual direction relationship in a variety of ways, especially by: a) self-care, wisely balancing time for worship, work, leisure, family, and personal relationships; b) addressing the difficulties multiple roles or relationships pose to the effectiveness or clarity of the spiritual direction relationship; c) removing oneself from any situation that compromises the integrity of the spiritual direction relationship.

5. Limitations. Spiritual directors recognize the limits of: a) energy, by restricting the number of directees; b) attentiveness, by appropriate spacing of meetings and directees; c) competence, by referring directees to other appropriately qualified persons when necessary.

II. THE SPIRITUAL DIRECTOR AND THE DIRECTEE

1. Covenant. Spiritual directors initiate conversation and establish agreements with directees about: a) the nature of spiritual direction; b) the roles of the director and the directee; c) the length and frequency of direction sessions; d) the compensation, if any, to be given to the director or institution; e) the process for evaluating and terminating the relationship.

2. Dignity. Spiritual directors honor the dignity of the directee by: a) respecting the directee's values, conscience, spirituality, and theology; b) inquiring into the motives, experiences, or relationships of the directee only as necessary; c) recognizing the imbalance of power in the spiritual direction relationship and taking care not to exploit it; d) establishing and maintaining appropriate physical and psychological boundaries with the directee; e) refraining from sexualized behavior, including, but not limited to, manipulative, abusive, or coercive words or actions toward a directee.

3. Confidentiality. Spiritual directors maintain the confidentiality and the privacy of the directee by: a) protecting the identity of the directee; b) keeping confidential all oral and written matters arising in the spiritual direction sessions; c) conducting direction sessions in appropriate settings; d) addressing legal regulations requiring disclosure to proper authorities, including but not limited to, child abuse, elder abuse, and physical harm to self and others.

III. THE SPIRITUAL DIRECTOR AND OTHERS

1. Colleagues. Spiritual directors maintain collegial relationships with ministers and professionals by: a) developing intra- and interdisciplinary relationships; b) requesting a directee who is in therapy to inform his or her therapist about being in spiritual direction; c) securing written releases and permission from directees when specific information needs to be shared for the benefit of the directee; d) respecting ministers and professionals by not disparaging them or their work.

2. Faith Communities. Spiritual directors maintain responsible relationships to communities of faith by: a) remaining open to processes of corporate discernment, accountability, and support; b) appropriately drawing on the teachings and practices of communities of faith; c) respecting the directee's relationship to his or her own community of faith.

3. Society. Spiritual directors, when presenting themselves to the public, preserve the integrity of spiritual direction by: a) representing qualifications and affiliations accurately; b) defining the particular nature and purpose of spiritual direction; c) respecting all persons regardless of race, color, sex, sexual orientation, age, religion, national origin, marital status, political belief, mental or physical handicap, any preference, personal characteristic, condition or status.

APPENDIX B

BASIC INDICATORS OF A HEALTHY SPIRITUAL DIRECTOR

by Teresa Blythe, included and adapted by permission

Culled from the Ethical Guidelines, *A Code of Ethics for Spiritual Directors* and the lived experience of many spiritual directors, here are some signs of a healthy spiritual director:

- Listens for the client's sacred truth and respects it.
- Does not try to push the client in one direction or another.
- Honors the client's spiritual or religious background.
- Maintains confidentiality.
- Respects physical, emotional and spiritual boundaries.
- Prays/meditates as a way of life.
- Pursues continuing education in the field of spiritual direction.
- Maintains good relationship with other spiritual directors.
- Wants the client to discover, for himself or herself, how the Divine is present in his or her life.
- Makes sure the meeting space is private and safe.

- Offers referrals when the client needs assistance that goes beyond spiritual direction.
- Ensures that the direction session is always about the client—not about the director.
- Begins on time and ends on time, respecting the schedule.
- Is careful to avoid developing a "dual" relationship with the client. In other words, makes sure that the only role he or she plays in the life of the client is that of spiritual director.

APPENDIX C

BASIC INDICATORS OF AN UNHEALTHY SPIRITUAL DIRECTOR

by Teresa Blythe, included and adapted by permission

- Doesn't listen.
- Makes judgmental comments.
- Pushes the client in one direction or another.
- Does not respect the client's spiritual or religious background.
- Breaks confidentiality.
- Violates boundaries with inappropriate comments or touch.
- Has abandoned his or her own spiritual practices and path.
- Talks about himself or herself too much.
- Allows the session to get into a mode where he or she is "fixing" the client's "problems."
- Allows interruptions—by phone or people "dropping in" while the session is going on.
- Misses appointments without advance notice, starts late and does not end on time.
- Initiates a relationship outside of the direction session.

Examples include trying to sell you something, advocating on the client's behalf without being asked for such support, becoming their special friend.

- Displays a callous, rude or indifferent attitude toward what is shared.
- Falls asleep (believe it or not, people tell me this has happened to them!)

ABOUT THE AUTHOR

The Rev. John R. Mabry, PhD is the author of more than twenty books, many of them on spirituality and spiritual direction. He is a United Church of Christ pastor and serves as director of the Interfaith Spiritual Direction Certificate Program at the Chaplaincy Institute in Berkeley, CA. He lives with his wife Lisa and numerous dogs in Oakland, California.

For a free book, visit John's website at:
www.johnrmabry.com

.

16306178R00062

Printed in Great Britain
by Amazon